BODY IMAGE DISTURBANCE

Assessment and Treatment

J. KEVIN THOMPSON
University of South Florida

PERGAMON PRESS
Member of Maxwell Macmillan Pergamon Publishing Corporation
New York • Oxford • Beijing • Frankfurt
São Paulo • Sydney • Tokyo • Toronto

Pergamon Press Offices:

U.S.A. Pergamon Press, Inc., Maxwell House, Fairview Park,
Elmsford, New York 10523, U.S.A.

U.K. Pergamon Press plc, Headington Hill Hall,
Oxford OX3 0BW, England

PEOPLE'S REPUBLIC Pergamon Press, Room 4037, Qianmen Hotel, Beijing,
OF CHINA People's Republic of China

FEDERAL REPUBLIC Pergamon Press GmbH, Hammerweg 6,
OF GERMANY D-6242 Kronberg, Federal Republic of Germany

BRAZIL Pergamon Editora Ltda, Rua Eça de Queiros, 346,
CEP 04011, São Paulo, Brazil

AUSTRALIA Pergamon Press Australia Pty Ltd., P.O. Box 544,
Potts Point, NSW 2011, Australia

JAPAN Pergamon Press, 8th Floor, Matsuoka Central Building,
1-7-1 Nishishinjuku, Shinjuku-ku, Tokyo 160, Japan

CANADA Pergamon Press Canada Ltd., Suite 271, 253 College Street,
Toronto, Ontario M5T 1R5, Canada

Copyright © 1990 Pergamon Press, Inc.

Library of Congress Cataloging in Publication Data

Thompson, J. Kevin.
    Body image disturbance : assessment and treatment / by J. Kevin
Thompson.
        p.   cm. -- (Psychology practitioner guidebooks)
        ISBN 0-08-036822-0 :   -- ISBN 0-08-036821-2 (pbk.) :
        1. Anorexia nervosa. 2. Body image. 3. Self-acceptance.
    I. Title. II. Series.
    RC552.A5T49   1990
    616.85'2--dc20   89-39663
                                                          CIP

Printed in the United States of America

The paper used in this publication meets the minimum requirements of
American National Standard for Information Sciences -- Permanence of
Paper for Printed Library Materials, ANSI Z39.48-1984

Dedication

Dedicated to the memory of Walt Isaac and Norm Schultz—two individuals who taught me much about psychology, but more about life.

Contents

Foreword

The historical roots of the concept of body image are firmly implanted in clinical practice. Around the turn of the century, clinicians, especially neurologists, struggled to understand their patients' reports of bizarre body experiences. From the examining rooms of seldom remembered clinicians like Bonnier, Pick, Head, Poetzl, Pineas, and Gerstmann, there emerged Cartesian puzzles of mind-body connections—body experiences (e.g., phantom limbs) that were incongruent with physical or observational realities. Though we may have forgotten these clinical origins, nonetheless our professional pursuits to comprehend the body experience and its relation to problems in human living certainly continue. Dr. Thompson's present volume articulates these pursuits and gives the reader a contemporary sense of the states of both our knowledge and our ignorance about this phenomenon called "body image."

Ten years ago, body image was not particularly a "hot topic" in either psychological science or clinical practice. Were it not for our awareness of the "epidemic" of eating disorders, I doubt if there would be the extant, heightened interest in body image—even though psychologist–scholars like Schilder, Fisher, Secord and Jourard, and Shontz consistently tried to capture our interest. For better or for worse, eating disorders are putting body image on the map of psychological inquiry. The good news is the improvement in our assessment of "body image" and related conceptual developments. The bad news ultimately would be reflected in the parochialism of inquiry and practice—that body image becomes overly identified with eating disorders rather than considered in its own right, clinically and nonclinically.

Personally, although a clinical psychologist, I entered the body-image realm through a different door—the largely social psychological door of physical appearance research. Years ago, studying the influences of objective physical attractiveness on human development and relations, I came to realize that persons' perceptions and emotions vis-a-vis their own physical appearance were quite different from "objective" (social consensual) realities. These "insider" (self-perception) and "outsider" (social perception) views of physical appearance/aesthetics typically share less than ten percent variance. Clearly, beauty is no guarantee of a positive body image, nor is homeliness a certain predictor of an unhappy body image. As a result of this understanding, I considerably shifted my research program to attempt to understand this discrepancy and the more important role of self-perceived appearance in everyday life. My interest in eating disorders came much later.

Not only does the present work reflect this zeitgeist of body-image theory, research, and practice in relation to eating disturbances, but Dr. Thompson offers information and insights that can take us beyond this singular focus. Among the most resonant themes of his guidebook is the multidimensionality of the body-image construct. Like many of us who have striven to articulate the components of the construct, Dr. Thompson argues for the essential distinction between perceptual (size estimation) and subjective (attitudinal) components or modalities of body image. Moreover, he delineates potentially important distinctions within each of these modalities. This sophistication is needed, whether one approaches the topic as a behavioral scientist or as a clinical practitioner. Dr. Thompson will not permit us to simplify body image, rather we must first discern which facet of body image we wish to describe, assess, explain, or modify.

The surge of interest in body image has produced myriad assessment techniques and inventories. Assessment choices necessitate decisions dependent on conceptual and psychometric as well as pragmatic issues. Yet the decision-making process can be as confusing and conflictual and as consequential as that of purchasing a new car. This book is uniquely useful, providing something of a "Consumer Reports" for body-image assessment. Dr. Thompson organizes our thinking and our priorities and gives us data on which we can base rational choices—before we take the assessment vehicle on our own road test.

With the advent of DSM-III-R's "Body Dysmorphic Disorder" comes the opportunity to expand our understanding of distorted and dysfunctional body experiences. For many years, cosmetic surgeons have grappled with the dysphoric preoccupations of surgery-seeking patients who are convinced that they are hideously disfigured (despite the absence of concurrence in "objective," socially perceived, reality). As I argued above, limiting our body-image inquiries to eating disorders needlessly narrows our knowledge of body image. My hope is that Dr. Thompson's devotion of an entire, albeit unfortunately brief, chapter to the clinical phenenomenon of body dysmorphic disorders will capture the curiosity and creativitiy of scientist-practitioners.

Should we be surprised that persons suffer from unhappy or distorted experiences of their own physical appearance? Each of us transacts with a cultural context that consistently conveys that "books *are* judged by their covers." For some of us, especially females, these transactions can be powerfully pathogenic. In aptly articulating these contexts of culture and gender, Dr. Thompson enhances our understanding of such distal causal forces in addition to the more proximal functional relationships among body-image percepts, affects, cognitions, and behaviors.

Systematic efforts to intervene and ameliorate dysfunctional body images are in their infancy. While controlled investigations of body-image therapies are few, innovative ideas abound. In his detailed discussion of body-image interventions, Dr. Thompson employs scientific rigor in designing and evaluating treatment studies. More importantly, I think, he takes us beyond *F* ratios and control groups in his mindful eclecticism for clinical practice.

I am convinced that body image can be a useful construct—meaningful to the researcher, to the practitioner, and ultimately to the individual. However, its utility relies on the coherent comprehension of its conceptual structure and boundaries, its multidimensionality, its reliable and valid measurement, and its therapeutic plasticity. In these significant matters, the present guidebook indeed guides.

Thomas F. Cash, Ph.D.
Professor of Psychology
Old Dominion University
Norfolk, Virginia

Preface

Research and clinical work in the area of body image disturbance is now proceeding at a phenomenal pace. Once located firmly within the domain of the field of eating disorders, body image has clearly transcended those narrow borders. Currently, research into the perceptual and subjective components of physical appearance-related body image disturbance includes basic as well as applied investigations. A number of populations are being vigorously studied, including, nonclinical adults and adolescents, athletes, obese individuals, and eating-disordered populations. These data indicate that body image disturbance is associated with several clinically relevant variables, including depression, low self-esteem, and general psychological dysfunction. This book provides a broad overview of prevalence data and associated features of body image dysfunction in the populations mentioned above. In addition, it offers a thorough examination of theoretical models, with a focus on the sociocultural approach.

However, the major purpose of this book is to provide a comprehensive, empirically documented, description of assessment and treatment methodologies for various aspects of body image disturbance. Despite the relative infancy of this field, research has been of a very high quality, offering some firm guidelines for measurement and intervention. There is much, however, that we do not know about the assessment and treatment of some populations. Therefore, I have also provided practical illustrations and case examples with a focus on the individualization of treatment regimens.

Chapters 1–3 are quite research-oriented, while Chapters 4–6 are heavily weighted toward application with clinical populations. For a full appreciation of the complexity of body image disturbance, I would recommend that the book be read sequentially, even by those individ-

uals who are most interested in applied issues. There are many ave-
nues for future exploration, and I have noted these for the individual
who would like to pursue body image research. Unfortunately, as I
note in Chapter 7, there appears to be no end to the societal view that,
at least for women, "thinness equals attractiveness"; therefore, I fore-
see an expanding role into the 1990s for the researcher and clinician
interested in the assessment and treatment of body image disturbance.

Acknowledgments

There are many individuals who made the writing of this book possible. First, I would like to acknowledge the colleagues who collaborated with me on various investigations of body image disturbance. While at the University of Alabama at Birmingham, I had the pleasure of working with Jeffrey Dolce, Nancy Berland, Roland Weinsier, Beth Jacobs, Patrick Linton, Paul Blanton, Angela Register, and Jim Raczynski. Colleagues at the University of South Florida include Dale Coovert, Larry Pasman, Lisa Fabian, Debbie Goldsmith, Lynda Scalf-McIver, Glenda Stelnicki, Rick Spana, Jim Connelly, Kevin Richards, David Reed, Madeline Altabe, Leah Postelnik, Kay Psaltis, Desiree Moulton, Jenny Robb, Paula Johnstone, Doug Stimac, Karen McDonald, Leslie Heinberg, and Bill Kinder. Special thanks to Lou Penner, for his close collaboration and role in directing my research career. Appreciation also goes to Winnie Rockman, who handled much of the technical work, including, typing, printing, and correspondence.

Other individuals, in many different ways, also played a strong role in the creation of this book. Leonard Epstein and John Martin initially generated my interested in psychology. Karen Calhoun, Ben Lahey, Rex Forehand, and Henry Adams had a powerful influence on my training, during the formative stages of my career. Bill Graziano constantly reminded me to do "quality" work, and his impact will always be felt. Mark Goldman challenged me to prove the importance of body image as a psychological construct. Frank Collins continues, after all these years, to be a source of innovation. Billy Barrios and Gary Ruff created the prototype of the measurement instrument that would be used in much of my research. Thomas Cash provided a strong role model and guide for someone new to this research area. Don Williams has served as a confidant and catalyst for many of the ideas that led to productive conclusions. Colleen Johnston collaborated on one of the most important research studies—her insights and support have been invaluable. In addition, thanks to Greg Jarvie, Blake Tearnan, Cindy Baum, and Joel Haber for the excitement of the early days of research.

Finally, my greatest thanks go to my parents and brothers. Their strength and unconditional support have given me the inspiration for all that I've accomplished. I hope they are as proud of me as I am of them.

Chapter 1

Body Image Disturbance: Overview of the Problem

DEFINITIONS OF BODY IMAGE

The construct of "body image" has been used to describe various phenomena that vary widely in their specific characteristics. The definitions of body image used by researchers in the area are very idiosyncratic to the particular type of body image under investigation (Thompson, Penner, & Altabe, 1990). This book deals specifically with the physical appearance-related aspect of body image and its subcomponents. However, it is instructive to review other definitions of body image that have been used to define related fields of study.

For instance, in neurological and neuropsychological circles, researchers have found that a perturbation in cortical functioning may lead to the failure to perceive that a part of the body belongs to the self (anosognosia). Another type of disturbance involves the actual removal of a part of the body without a corresponding realization of the loss—the phantom limb phenomenon (Lacey & Birtchnell, 1986; McCrea, Summerfield, & Rosen, 1982; Shontz, 1974). Psychoanalytic theory has profited richly from a "body boundary" conceptualization of body image, a concept introduced by Fisher (1986) who noted that people vary "with respect to the firmness or definiteness they ascribe to their body boundaries" (p. 329). These definitions, along with other formulations of body image, are clearly distinct from a physical appearance-related formulation.

The essential feature of the physical appearance definition of body image is an evaluation of one's size, weight, or any other aspect of the body that determines physical appearance. Generally, researchers and clinicians subdivide the physical appearance construct into three areas:

a perceptual component, commonly referred to as size perception accuracy (estimation of body size); a subjective component, which deals with facets such as satisfaction, concern, cognitive evaluation, and anxiety; and a behavioral component, which focuses on avoidance of situations that cause the individual to experience physical appearance-related discomfort.

In some cases, the disturbance of a physical appearance-related aspect of body image can be extremely severe. When the body image disparagement reaches these proportions, the phenomenon has been labeled dysmorphophobia (Hay, 1970; Lacey & Birtchnell, 1986). This clinical entity was recently named Body Dysmorphic Disorder and included in the *Diagnostic and Statistical Manual of Mental Disorders* 3rd ed., rev., (DSM-III-R) under the category of Somatoform Disorders (American Psychiatric Association, 1987). The outstanding characteristic of this disorder is an individual's subjective aversion of a particular part of the body which appears normal to an observer.

This book presents a broad overview of the physical appearance type of body image disturbance. Therefore, for our purposes, any use of the phrase "body image" is relegated to this singular definition of the construct. Historically, research has focused on the investigation of body image and its accompanying disturbances with eating disordered populations (Thompson et al., 1990). However, the great majority of recent research has dealt with nonclinical populations. The historical progression from the early detection of disturbance in anorexia nervosa to a current analysis of the "normative discontent" (Rodin, Silberstein, & Striegel-Moore, 1984, p. 267) in the general population is presented next. Subsequent chapters fully evaluate the significance of body image disturbance in clinical and nonclinical samples, with a special focus on theoretical models, assessment measures, and treatment procedures. In addition, as will become apparent, body image disturbance is largely a phenomenon that affects female members of the population; therefore, with few exceptions, the patient and subject samples referred to throughout this book consist of females.

EARLY DETECTION IN
ANOREXIA NERVOSA

Lasegue (1873, cited in Touyz & Beumont, 1987) was the first individual to comment on the relevance of body image disturbance to anorexia nervosa. His patient noted that she was "neither changed nor thinner" (Touyz & Beumont, 1987, p. 172) when confronted with the fact that her food intake could not support a young infant. The relevance of this aspect of anorexia nervosa to an understanding of the complete phenomenon of eating-disordered behavior was formulated much later by Hilde Bruch (1962), who was the first researcher to postulate a developmental model of anorexia nervosa. Bruch described three key symptoms as necessary for the development of the disorder, and body image disturbance was one of the triumvirate.

She was taken by the seeming lack of concern of patients toward their emaciated appearance, noting that the cardinal pathognomic feature of anorexia nervosa was not the emaciation "but rather the distortion of body image associated with it . . . and the vigor and stubbornness with which the often gruesome appearance is defended as normal and right, *not* too thin" (Bruch, 1962, p. 189). She also thought that patients might "gain weight for many reasons" but "without a corrective change in the body image, however, the improvement is apt to be only a temporary remission" (p. 189).

Bruch's theory received strong empirical support when Slade and Russell (1973) found that anorexics actually overestimated the size of their body to a greater degree than control subjects. In this classic study, they used an apparatus that required subjects to adjust the width between two lights mounted on a movable track to match that of their own estimate of the distance of a specific body site. In addition to the overestimation of body size that was found for the anorexics, it was noted that the level of overestimation decreased as patients gained weight and was related to relapse following their discharge from the hospital.

Following this study, other researchers replicated their results (for reviews see Cash & Brown, 1987; Garner & Garfinkel, 1981; Slade, 1985; Thompson et al., 1990) and the criteria of body image disturbance came to be included in the *Diagnostic and Statistical Manual of Mental Disorders, 3rd ed.*, (DSM-III) of the American Psychiatric Association (1980) as one of five diagnostic criteria necessary for the diagnosis of anorexia nervosa. In the early 1980s, a relatively new eating disorder, bulimia nervosa, emerged, and researchers turned their attention to the assessment of body image in this population. Their findings indicated that these individuals also experienced a significant amount of size estimation inaccuracy, possibly overestimating to a greater degree than anorexics (Thompson, Berland, Linton, & Weinsier, 1986). This led researchers to include body image disturbance as a diagnostic criteria for the diagnosis of bulimia nervosa in DSM-III-R (American Psychiatric Association, 1987). Table 1.1 contains the current diagnostic criteria, including body image disturbance, for anorexia nervosa and bulimia nervosa.

Table 1.1. Diagnostic criteria for anorexia nervosa and bulimia nervosa

---

Anorexia Nervosa

A. Refusal to maintain body weight over a minimal normal weight for age and height, e.g., weight loss leading to maintenance of body weight 15% below that expected; or failure to make expected weight gain during a period of growth, leading to body weight 15% below that expected.

B. Intense fear of gaining weight or becoming fat, even though underweight.

C. Disturbance in the way in which one's body weight, size, or shape is experienced, e.g., the person claims to "feel fat" even when emaciated, believes that one area of the body is "too fat" even when obviously underweight.

D. In females, absence of at least three consecutive menstrual cycles when otherwise expected to occur (primary or secondary amenorrhea). (A woman is considered to have amenorrhea if her periods occur only following hormone, e.g., estrogen, administration.)

Bulimia Nervosa

A. Recurrent episodes of binge eating (rapid consumption of a large amount of food in a discrete period of time.)

B. A feeling of lack of control over eating behavior during the eating binges.

C. The person regularly engages in either self-induced vomiting, use of laxatives or diuretics, strict dieting or fasting, or vigorous exercise in order to prevent weight gain.

D. A minimum average of two binge eating episodes a week for at lest three months.

E. Persistent overconcern with body shape and weight.

Reprinted with permission from the *Diagnostic and Statistical Manual of Mental Disorders, Third Edition, Revised.* Copyright 1987 American Psychiatric Association.

CURRENT EVIDENCE IN GENERAL POPULATION: A "NORMATIVE DISCONTENT"

During this same time period, in the early 1980s, various researchers began to catalog the frequency of body image disturbance in nonclinical populations (Rodin et al., 1984). Several investigations have clearly documented the prevalence of disturbance in non-eating-disordered subjects, but perhaps a few large-scale surveys best indicate the level of unhappiness with body image present in the general population.

In one of the first studies to sample a large portion of the population, Nielsen (1979) found that 56% of all females (aged 24–54) were on a diet. Wooley and Wooley (1984) found that 63% of the women in their survey stated that weight often affected how they felt about themselves; 33% reported that it sometimes affected their feelings; and only 4% stated that it never had any impact on how they felt about themselves. Silberstein, Striegel-Moore, and Rodin (1987), in a longitudinal study of women over the age of 62, found that fear of weight gain was their second greatest concern—memory loss was first. Hatfield and Sprecher (1986) noted that a survey of sexual practices by Kinsey and co-workers revealed that women were more embarrassed when questioned about their weight than about sexual activities such as frequency of masturbation.

Cash, Winstead, and Janda (1986), in a nationwide survey of 30,000 individuals (a sample of 2,000 was analyzed, in order to accurately represent the adult population, by gender and age), found high levels of dissatisfaction with body image in females and males. Only 18% of the men they surveyed and 7% of the women expressed little concern with their appearance. A comparison of the 1986 figures with a previous survey conducted in 1972 revealed an increase in dissatisfaction for both genders (see Table 1.2). However, women are currently more unhappy than men in all body areas except the face and height.

Cash et al. (1986) also found that women scored lower on overall physical appearance evaluation than men. Twenty-four percent of the men rated their physical appearance negative, whereas, 31% of the women gave an overall negative rating on this attribute. Women also scored more negatively than men on scales designed to assess their own evaluation of their fitness, health, and sexuality. Subjects also rated their own subjective weight category, and this assignment was compared to an objective weight index, derived by comparing their own weight and height to those of established norms. The results revealed that men were more accurate at categorizing themselves than women. Underweight women were more likely than men to consider them-

Table 1.2. Body satisfaction levels for males and females—1972 vs. 1986

	1972 Survey			1985 Survey	
	Men	Women		Men	Women
Height	13%	13%	Height	20%	17%
Weight	35	48	Weight	41	55
Muscle Tone	25	30	Muscle Tone	32	45
Overall Face	8	11	Face	20	20
Breast/Chest	18	26	Upper Torso	28	32
Abdomen	36	50	Mid Torso	50	57
Hips and Upper			Lower Torso	21	50
Thighs	12	49	"Looks As		
Overall			They Are"	34	38
Appearance	15	25			

selves as fitting the normal-weight designation, and normal-weight women were more likely to assign themselves to the overweight category. For instance, as Table 1.3 indicates, 47% of the objectively normal-weight women placed themselves in the overweight category; 40% of the underweight women put themselves in the normal-weight range.

Recent data with non-eating disordered subjects has also documented the size overestimation found previously with anorexic and bulimic samples (Birtchnell, Dolan, & Lacey, 1987). For example, Thompson (1986), found that approximately 95% of women overestimated the size of their bodies. The waist was overestimated to the greatest degree (35%), followed by the hips (17%) and thighs (11%) (Thompson & Spana, 1988). Thompson and Thompson (1986) noted that overestimation for females was approximately twice that of males. Adolescent populations have also been found to overestimate body sizes (Fabian & Thompson, 1989). In fact, recent reviews have concluded that size overestimation is certainly not specific to eating-disordered populations (Cash & Brown, 1987; Garner, Garfinkel, & Bonato, 1987; Hsu, 1982; Slade, 1985). (This issue is examined further in Chapter 2).

Therefore, it is apparent that serious, clinically relevant body image dysfunction now exists in non-eating-disordered populations. The recognition of this relatively new clinical entity has led researchers to conduct treatment investigations focused narrowly on body image problems in normal populations (Butters & Cash, 1987; Rosen, Saltzberg, & Srebnik, 1989). In addition, researchers have begun to document evidence in support of the damaging effects of body image disturbance on general psychological functioning. For instance, researchers have discovered strong associations between perceptual and subjective aspects of disturbance and lowered self-esteem, elevated depression, and general psychological distress (for a review, see Thompson et al., 1990).

Rodin and colleagues have noted that women's concern with weight and body image has reached such proportions that "it can be con-

Table 1.3. Self-perceived weight categorization versus objective weight placement

Self-perceived Weight Category	Men			Women		
	Under-weight	Normal weight	Over-weight	Under-weight	Normal weight	Over-weight
Under	90%	16%	1%	56%	6%	0%
Normal	10	55	9	40	47	0
Over	0	29	90	4	47	100

From T. F. Cash, B. A. Winstead, & L. H. Janda (April, 1986). Body image survey report: The great American shape-up. *Psychology Today, 20,* p. 36, Table 3. Reprinted with permission from Psychology Today Magazine. Copyright © *1986* (PT Partners, L.P.).

sidered a normal part of the female experience" (Silberstein et al., 1987, p. 89). As noted earlier, they coined the phrase "normative discontent" (Rodin et al., 1984, p. 267) to describe the pervasiveness of this problem. Indeed, they view this normative discontent with body image as existing on a continuum. Individuals at the extreme end of the scale who experience high levels of disturbance have an elevated risk for developing eating disorders. Unfortunately, all evidence indicates that these levels of body image distress will probably continue to rise in the near future (Hsu, 1989; Silberstein et al., 1987).

SUMMARY

The preceding historical overview briefly captures the evolution of body image disturbance, from its founding association with anorexia nervosa to its more recent localization in bulimia nervosa and non-eating-disordered women. Several theoretical explanations have been offered to explain the occurrence of body image dysfunction and the increase in disturbance during the current generation, particularly its primary locus in the female population. These theories are explored in Chapter 3. However, prior to a discussion of causal factors, the next chapter first offers a fuller examination of the depths of body image disturbance in different population groups. In addition, the relationships between aspects of physical appearance disturbance and other facets of psychological functioning (for instance, eating disturbance, self-esteem, depression, etc.) are reviewed.

Chapter 2

Body Image Disturbance in Various Populations: Extent of Disturbance and Associated Features

The last chapter offered a historical perspective that provided an overview of body image disturbance in eating-disordered and non-eating-disordered populations. As mentioned earlier, the great majority of this book deals with body image disturbance among adult women—the group that appears to be at greatest risk. However, researchers are increasingly turning their attention to an investigation of various other population groups, including men, adolescents, athletes, ballet dancers, and obese individuals. In addition, the extent and specific type of disturbance in eating-disordered populations is receiving renewed scrutiny. Research has also begun to focus on the significance of body image disturbance by examining its relationship to general psychological functioning (self-esteem, depression, level of eating disturbance) and its role as a causal factor in the development of eating disorders. This chapter examines the prevalence and correlates of different aspects of physical appearance-related body image disturbance in various populations.

ADULTS

Extent of Disturbance

Currently, researchers have turned their efforts toward understanding the many subtleties of adults' body image disturbance. As outlined in the previous chapter, there is now general agreement that a large degree of dysfunction exists, particularly in the areas of subjective happiness with body size, weight, and appearance. In the past few years, researchers have focused on the many different components of subjective and perceptual body image disturbance. In this area, the issue of gender differences has received a good deal of attention.

Fallon and Rozin (1985), in a seminal investigation of body image disturbance, had males and females pick their figures from a range of schematic drawings that included very thin to very fat choices. All subjects were asked to indicate their current figure, their ideal figure, the figure they thought would be most attractive to the opposite sex, and the opposite sex figure that they found most attractive. Men's current figure, their ideal size, and the figure they thought would be most attractive to women were almost identical. However, women's choice of their current figure was larger than the figure they thought would be most appealing to men which, in turn, was also larger than their ideal figure. The results of this study are shown in Figure 2.1.

Interestingly, the males' selection of the male figure they thought most attractive to women was larger than the figure that women actually selected as the most attractive male size—men appear to think that women like a larger male figure than they actually do. Finally, women's selection of the figure that they thought most attractive to men was smaller than the figure that men actually chose as the female figure they most liked—men like a larger female figure than women think they do. The authors concluded that "men's perceptions serve to keep them satisfied with their figures, whereas women's perceptions place pressure on them to lose weight" (Fallon & Rozin, 1985, p. 102).

In a replication and extension of Fallon and Rozin's (1985) findings with females, Thompson and Psaltis (1988) had college females rate their current size, using the same figure-rating scale as the previous authors; however, the instructional format was changed to differentiate an affective from a cognitive rating. Specifically, subjects were asked to choose the figure that illustrated "how you *think* you currently look" and "how you *feel* most of the time" (p. 814). They also rated their ideal figure, how they thought others saw them, and the size they thought would be most attractive to men. The findings indicated that the figure chosen based on how they felt about their current size was larger than any of the other selections, including how they thought they looked. There was no difference, however, between how they thought they looked and how they thought others saw them. Finally, ideal size and the size they thought most attractive to men were equivalent, but smaller than the other three figure ratings. These data are contained in Figure 2.2.

These findings emphasize the importance of the instructional format

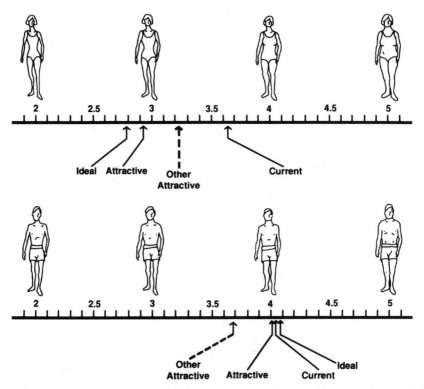

FIGURE 2.1. Mean ratings by women (top) and men (bottom) of current figure, ideal figure, and figure most attractive to the opposite sex: mean ratings by men of the female figure that they find most attractive (top, labeled "Other Attractive") and equivalent mean ratings by women, on the bottom. (Sample: college students, ages unspecified.)

From A. E. Fallon & P. Rozin. (1985). Sex differences in perceptions of desirable body shape. *Journal of Abnormal Psychology, 94,* 103, Figure 1. Figures originally printed in "Use of the Danish Adoption Register for the Study of Obesity and Thinness" by A. J. Stunkard, T. Sorensen, and F. Schulsinger, 1983, in *The Genetics of Neurological and Psychiatric Disorders* (pp. 115–120). New York: Raven Press. Copyright 1983 by Raven Press. Reprinted by permission.

when subjects are asked to select a current size rating. The affective component of figure selection can clearly be separated from a rational, cognitively based estimate of size. Subjects' rating of how they *thought* they looked was, in fact, no different from how they thought they appeared to others (Thompson & Psaltis, 1988). They *felt*, however, larger than how they thought others saw them.

Using a different methodology, Thompson and Dolce (1989) recently replicated the Thompson and Psaltis (1988) study. Subjects were college females who used a size estimation procedure—the Adjustable Light Beam Apparatus (Thompson & Spana, 1988)—that requires subjects to adjust a light beam to match the size of specific body sites (in

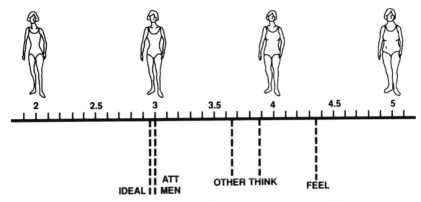

FIGURE 2.2 Mean ratings for women for ideal rating, how they *think* they look, how they *feel* they look, how others see their figure, and the figure they think is most attractive to men. (Sample: college females aged 17–25.)

Adapted from data presented in J. K. Thompson & K. Psaltis. (1988). Multiple aspects and correlates of human figure ratings. *International Journal of Eating Disorders, 7,* 813–817. Figures originally printed in "Use of the Danish Adoption Register for the Study of Obesity and Thinness" by A. J. Stunkard, T. Sorensen, and F. Schulsinger, 1983, in *The Genetics of Neurological and Psychiatric Disorders* (pp. 115–120). New York: Raven Press. Copyright 1983 by Raven Press. Reprinted by permission.

this study, waist, hips, and thighs). Rather than simply asking subjects to match the light beam width to their own estimate of the width of a specific body site (the usual procedure) subjects were asked to rate their widths utilizing the affective and cognitive rating protocols mentioned above. They also chose the light beam that matched their conception of their ideal size and the ideal for other women of their same height and frame size (this was included to test whether their own requirements of a body size were more rigid than those they held for other women). After ratings were taken, subjects' actual sizes were measured with body calipers; thus, actual size was also entered as a rating in the analyses.

In this study, sizes based on affective instructions were larger than those selected via cognitive ratings, but the differences were not significant. However, affective sizes were significantly larger than all other ratings, including the subjects' actual sizes. Estimates based on cognitive instructions were, however, no different than the subjects' actual sizes, but were larger than their ideal size and the ideal rating of others' sizes. Actual, ideal self, and ideal other ratings did not differ. These findings are presented in Table 2.1.

In an attempt to evaluate generational and gender effects on body image, Rozin and Fallon (1988), using their previous methodology, had college males and females and their biological parents choose figure ratings. Subjects also completed several single questions that ad-

Table 2.1. Means, standard deviations, significance levels, and percentage
overestimation/underestimation for various size ratings (Sample: college females:
ages 17–35). Means that share a common letter are not significantly different. Numbers
are in centimeters. Percentages indicate differences between adjacent ratings.

	Percentage Above Actual Size			Percentage Below Actual Size	
	16.0%			−9.2%	
	7.7%	8.3%	−3.7%	−5.5%	
	Emotional	Rational	Actual	Ideal Self	Ideal Other
Mean	34.54a	32.06ab	29.61bc	28.56c	27.07c
Standard Deviation	6.55	5.37	4.46	5.40	4.59

From J. K. Thompson & J. J. Dolce (1989). The discrepancy between emotional vs. rational estimates of body size, actual size, and ideal body ratings: Theoretical and clinical implications. *Journal of Clinical Psychology, 45,* 473–478. Copyright 1989 by *Journal of Clinical Psychology.* Reprinted by permission.

dressed their concern with weight and eating. Mothers, fathers, and daughters (but, not sons) rated their current shape as larger than their ideal. Both mothers and daughters thought that men of their own generation preferred smaller women than men actually rated as most attractive. Interestingly, fathers, although similar to mothers and daughters in their perception of overweight (current figure larger than ideal) were relatively unconcerned about their weight and eating (resembling the sons in this regard). The authors concluded that gender, rather than current-ideal discrepancy *or* generation, was the most important factor in concern about weight. Figure 2.3 presents these findings.

Other researchers have also addressed the specific quality and quantity of body image disturbance in males versus females. Drewnoski and Yee (1987) surveyed male and female freshmen college students and found that 85% of the women wanted to lose weight whereas only 40% of the men were interested in weight reduction. Paradoxically, 45% of the men wanted to *gain* weight. Males and females who wished to lose weight shared a negative view of their body and dissatisfaction with body weight. Using the previously mentioned figure-rating scale, Silberstein, Striegel-Moore, Timko, and Rodin (1988) replicated Drewnoski and Yee's (1987) findings. Subjects were asked to choose their ideal and current figures. Equal numbers of males (78.2%) and females (77.3%) chose an ideal figure that was different from their current size. However, men were as likely to choose an ideal figure that was heavier (43.4%) than their current size as one that was smaller (34.8%). Only *one* female subject (2.3%) wanted to be heavier, whereas the rest of those females who had a discrepancy between ideal and current size

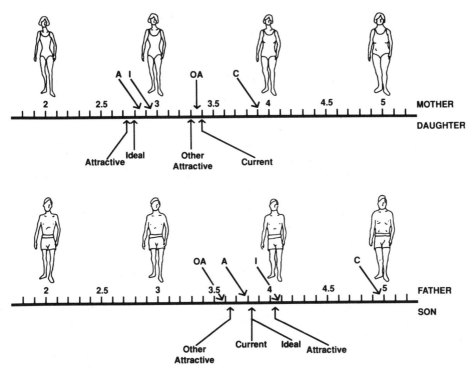

FIGURE 2.3. Mean ratings of current (C), ideal (I), most attractive to opposite sex (A), and most attractive to opposite sex as rated by the opposite sex (other attractive, OA). Part A, above top line: Ratings by mothers, except that other-attractive rating is of the most-attractive-mother figure, as rated by fathers. Part A, below top line, equivalent ratings by daughters. Part B corresponds exactly to Part A, but presents data from fathers and sons, with other-attractive ratings of male figures, as rated by mothers and daughters.

From P. Rozin & A. Fallon (1988). Body image, attitudes to weight, and misperceptions of figure preferences of the opposite sex: A comparison of men and women in two generations. *Journal of Abnormal Psychology, 97,* 343, Figure 2-1. Figures originally printed in "Use of the Danish Adoption Register for the Study of Obesity and Thinness" by A. J. Stunkard, T. Sorensen, and F. Schulsinger, 1983, in *The Genetics of Neurological and Psychiatric Disorders* (pp. 115–120). New York: Raven Press. Copyright 1983 by Raven Press. Reprinted by permission.

chose an ideal figure that was smaller. Essentially identical findings emerged when subjects were asked about weight satisfaction. An approximately equal number of males wanted to be thinner (40%) as wanted to be larger (46.8%). Only two (4.4%) of the females who were dissatisfied wanted to be larger—87% wanted to be thinner.

In a sample of college women and men, Hesse-Biber, Clayton-Matthews, and Downey (1988) found that 84.1% of the women wanted to lose weight versus 45% of the men. Women also wanted to lose an average of 10 pounds whereas, men wanted to lose less than 1 pound.

More than one-third of the women were unhappy with their body while less than one-tenth of the men were dissatisfied.

These studies serve to illustrate the large gender gap in subjective body dissatisfaction. Although relatively fewer investigators have measured size overestimation in non-eating disordered adults, some evidence suggests that females may overestimate body size to a larger degree than men. Thompson and Thompson (1986) evaluated 30 asymptomatic males and females, using the Adjustable Light Beam procedure (discussed earlier). Females averaged 25% overestimation, while the men were 14% above accuracy on their estimates of body size. Several other studies have found that female control subjects do not significantly differ from clinical anorexic samples in their degree of inaccuracy (discussed later in this chapter).

Correlates of Disturbance

Much research has addressed the connection between body image disturbance and eating dysfunction in nonclinical samples. Level of body image disturbance has also been shown to be connected to other aspects of general psychological disturbance, including depression, self-esteem, and teasing history. Interestingly, different aspects of body image dysfunction (perceptual vs. subjective) may be related in different ways to these associated features. These issues, beginning with the relationship between body image disturbance and general eating disturbance, are addressed next.

The expected strong connections between body image disturbance and eating disturbance, in non-eating-disordered populations, have been widely supported by empirical findings—with one exception. Results from studies that have correlated size overestimation and eating disturbance have been inconclusive. A brief overview of investigations that have evaluated the connection between subjective measures of body image disturbance and eating dysfunction is provided here, followed by a discussion of the conflicting results with the perceptual measures.

Almost without exception, subjective indices of appearance-related disturbance show high correlations with questionnaire indices of eating disturbance. Hesse-Biber et al. (1988) found that a self-rating of appearance evaluation was strongly associated with two measures of eating disturbance—the relation was more powerful for females than males. Silberstein et al. (1988) found that disordered eating in females was associated with lower overall body esteem and perceived-ideal body figure discrepancy (the authors noted that a skewed distribution of scores on the eating disturbance prohibited an analysis for men). Keeton, Cash, and Brown (in press), using a perceived-ideal discrepancy measure, also found a positive connection with eating disturbance, but only for females—no significant correlation existed for males.

Thompson and Psaltis (1988) found a negative relationship between physical appearance evaluation and a measure of bulimic behavior—college females with a more positive evaluation had less eating disturbance. This study also included a component that required subjects to choose a figure that matched their current and their ideal body sizes. Level of eating disturbance was positively related to perceived size (larger sizes were associated with greater disturbance), but not to ideal size.

The relationship between size overestimation and level of eating disturbance was evaluated by Coovert, Thompson, and Kinder (1988) who found no connection between the two measures. Similarly, Keeton et al. (in press) found no relationship between size overestimation and a measure of bulimic behavior. Therefore, it appears that size overestimation may have little relationship to eating disturbance in a normal population. However, as discussed later in this chapter, the issue may be quite different with individuals who have a diagnosed eating disorder.

There is also a wealth of data associating body image disturbance with depression. For instance, Marsella, Shizuru, Brennan, and Kameoka (1981) found that depressed college males and females had higher levels of subjective dissatisfaction with their body than nondepressed subjects. Noles, Cash, and Winstead (1985) replicated the Marsella et al. (1981) findings, also with male and female college students. However, in their study, the researchers videotaped each subject and had objective raters rate them on level of physical attractiveness. The depressed subjects were less satisfied with their bodies and rated themselves as less physically attractive than the nondepressed subjects; however, the objective ratings of attractiveness were equivalent for the groups. The authors concluded that Beck's inclusion of "distortion of body image" (Beck, 1973, p. 24) as a criteria for depression was supported. Thompson and Psaltis (1988) found a strong negative relationship between physical appearance evaluation and depression in a sample of college women—individuals with a poorer body image had a higher level of depression. Taylor and Cooper (1986) also found that size overestimation was positively related to level of depression.

In the area of self-esteem, the association of body image to ratings of aspects of the self has a long history. In the now classic study by Secord and Jourard (1953), ratings of body sites (body cathexis) were highly correlated with ratings of attributes of the overall self (self-cathexis). Hesse-Biber et al. (1988) found that a self-rating of attractiveness was negatively associated with self-ratings of self-confidence and self-acceptance, for both males and females. For females only, the attractiveness rating was related to low levels of intellectual self-confidence.

Silberstein et al. (1988) found that weight concern was *unrelated* to self-esteem in college women (interestingly, sexual attractiveness and physical condition were significantly correlated with self-esteem). The authors suggested that this odd finding might be explained by the possibility that "the normative nature of weight dissatisfaction for women today may serve to buffer its effects on self-esteem" (p. 219). Interestingly, they also found that the self-esteem scores of those women who wanted to be thinner were no different from those who had an ideal and a perceived figure that were congruent. Also, men's self-esteem was unaffected by whether they were heavier or thinner than they desired.

Little evidence exists on the relationship between self-esteem and size overestimation in non-eating-disordered populations. However, Thompson and Thompson (1986) found that high self-esteem was associated with lower size overestimation (greater accuracy), but only for females—the correlation for males was nonsignificant.

The great majority of research on the convergence between measures of body image and other variables has dealt with eating disturbance, depression, and self-esteem; however, a few researchers have looked at other variables. For instance, in college females, level of physical appearance evaluation and size of figure selection have been found to be positively associated with teasing history (Thompson and Psaltis, 1988). Specifically, the frequency of teasing during adolescence was negatively associated with physical appearance evaluation as an adult—more teasing led to poorer evaluation of body image. In addition, larger figure selections were associated with a greater history of teasing frequency and the negative effects of teasing (subjects rated the degree to which the teasing had adversely affected them). Table 2.2 contains the results of Thompson and Psaltis on the intercorrelations between physical appearance satisfaction and other measures.

Hesse-Biber et al. (1988) found that a self-rating of appearance evaluation was related to assertiveness, athletic ability, and self-understanding for males and females. However, for females, poorer body image was also associated with lower self-ratings for popularity, drive to achieve, public-speaking ability, originality, emotional maturity, and trustfulness. For males, but not for females, poor evaluation was related to low levels of sincerity. In a study that evaluated family processes and physical appearance evaluation, Scalf-McIver and Thompson (1989), in a sample of 175 college females, found that appearance evaluation was positively correlated with family cohesion, but nega-

Table 2.2. Relationships among figure ratings and other variables for college females (ages 17–25).

	Ideal Weight[a]	Think[b]	Feel[b]	Ideal[b]	Others[b]	Att. Men.[b]
Think[b]	.71**	—	—	—	—	—
Feel[b]	.60**	.77**	—	—	—	—
Ideal[b]	.27*	.41**	.13	—	—	—
Others[b]	.67*	.79**	.71**	.38**	—	—
Att. Men.[b]	.18	.29*	.69**	.76**	.21	—
T. F.[c]	−.08	.09	.09	−.06	−.10	−.03
T. E.[d]	.34**	.41**	.43**	.17	.45**	.15
BULIT[e]	.37**	.56**	.46**	.14	.42**	.06
BDI[f]	.07	.22	.30*	.08	.24	−.02
BSRQ-PAE[g]	−.37**	−.57**	−.60**	−.10	−.55**	.03
Age-Menarche[h]	−.21	−.12	−.20	.13	−.15	.14

	T. F.	T. E.	BULIT	BDI	BSRQ-PAE
T. E.[d]	.23	—	—	—	—
BULIT[e]	.38**	.40**	—	—	—
BDI[f]	.00	.06	.35**	—	—
BSRQ-PAE[g]	−.25*	−.41**	−.39**	−.41**	—
Age-Menarche[h]	−.14	−.10	−.02	−.07	−.23

From J. K. Thompson & K. Psaltis (1988). Multiple aspects and correlates of body figure ratings: A replication and extension of Fallon and Rozin (1985). *International Journal of Eating Disorders, 7*, 816, Table 1. Copyright © 1988 by John Wiley and Sons. Reprinted by permission of John Wiley and Sons, Inc.

[a] Ideal Weight = percentage determined by comparison with the midpoint of the range for medium build for each subject's height (Metropolitan Insurance Company, 1983).

[b] See description in text.

[c] Teasing Frequency.

[d] Teasing Effect.

[e] Bulimia Test.

[f] Beck Depression Inventory.

[g] Body-Self Relations Questionnaire—Physical Appearance Evaluation subscale (lower scores reflect greater dissatisfaction).

[h] Age of first menarche, in months.

*$p < .05$.

**$p < .01$.

tively related to family conflict. However, there was no relationship between appearance dissatisfaction and family control, mother inconsistency, or father inconsistency.

Keeton et al. (in press) looked at the connection between perceptual and subjective indices of disturbance and general psychological functioning, as measured with the SCL-90-R. Generally, there was a good deal of correspondence between several subjective indices of disturbance and global psychological functioning for both genders, indicating that increased body image disturbance was associated with poorer psychological functioning. In addition, for both males and females, size overestimation was also positively correlated with greater psychological disturbance. However, two discrepancy measures of ideal-perceived body sizes were unrelated to global functioning.

In summary, there appears to be a large degree of body image disturbance in the general population of adults, and this dysfunction is strongly connected with salient variables such as eating disturbance, depression, self-esteem, and general psychological functioning. The absolute level of the problem and its relationship to associated features appears to be stronger for females than for males. However, research in this area is hardly conclusive, especially in the area of self-esteem and body image disturbance in women, where an expected association has not always been located. In addition, the great majority of research has been conducted with college students, and whether these findings can be generalized to older adults, especially adult males, remains to be tested. Many of the above findings with adults have also been empirically replicated in adolescent populations and these data are discussed next.

ADOLESCENTS

Extent of Disturbance

Research in the area of body image disturbance in adolescents has proceeded at a vigorous pace in recent years. In many ways, the methodological sophistication in this area supersedes that of investigations with adults because longitudinal and causal modeling designs have been utilized and these permit researchers to make inferences regarding the causes of body image dysfunction.

Scattered studies have appeared throughout the past few decades (for a review see Whitaker, Davies, Shaffer, Johnson, Abrams, Walsh, & Kalikow, 1989) and this research has generally found that adolescent girls have more dissatisfaction with their bodies than boys. However, the real trend for many researchers to focus on body image in adolescents began in the early 1980s. As was the case with adults, the bulk of this research has focused on the subjective aspect of disturbance.

Tobin-Richards, Boxer, and Petersen (1983) found that girls perceive their overall body in more negative terms than boys. Davies and Furnham (1986a) found that less than 4% of a sample of British female adolescents (ages 12–18) were overweight as measured by standard charts, but over 10 times that number considered themselves overweight. Half of the sample wanted to lose weight. Eisele, Hertsgaard, and Light

(1986) found that 78% of their female adolescents preferred to weigh less, despite the fact that 81% were of normal weight according to weight charts. Davies and Furnham (1986b) found that satisfaction with body measurements decreased as girls' age increased from 12 to 18 years old. For example, unhappiness with the waist increased from 35% to 42%, and dissatisfaction with the hips went up substantially, from 22% to 62%.

Cohn, Adler, Irwin, Millstein, Kegeles, and Stone (1987) had a large number of male (283) and female (288) adolescents (ages: 10.5–15) pick body figures using the previously discussed figure-rating scales. Girls chose an ideal figure that was thinner than the figure they thought would be most attractive to boys; however, boys picked an ideal that was heavier than the one they thought would be most attractive to girls. Neither sex rated their current figure as significantly different from the figure they considered most attractive to the opposite gender.

Girls picked a current figure that was marginally (in statistical terms, almost significant) larger than their ideal figure while boys' ideal figure was significantly heavier than their current figure rating. Both groups erred when asked to pick the figure that appealed most to the opposite sex. Girls underestimated the size of the figure that was most preferred by boys, while boys chose a larger male figure than girls selected as the most attractive male figure. Therefore, these findings largely replicated the earlier work with adults (Fallon & Rozin, 1985), which documented gender differences in body dissatisfaction with the figure-rating procedure. Figure 2.4 contains the findings from Cohn et al. (1987).

Relatively few studies have investigated the level of size estimation accuracy in adolescents. Halmi, Goldberg, and Cunningham (1977) investigated size overestimation in 86 normal-weight adolescent girls and found that body size overestimation was greatest at the age of 10 (41%) and dropped gradually after that point (age 11 = 23%; age 18 = 11%). Fabian and Thompson (1989) did not find an age effect, although their sample's age range was more constricted (10–15). Subjects were dichotomized into premenarcheal and postmenarcheal, with mean ages of 11.3 and 13.3 respectively. Mean overestimation levels did not significantly differ as a result of pubertal status (premenarcheal = 21.5%; postmenarcheal = 18%). These findings held up when subjects within each menarcheal epoch were age matched.

Correlates of Disturbance

Recent work on the relationships between aspects of body image dysfunction and other variables has been quite constructive. As was the case with adults, subjective aspects of disturbance are highly cor-

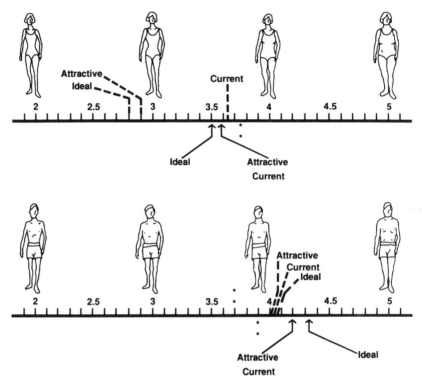

FIGURE 2.4. Mean figure ratings of adolescent girls (top figure, solid lines) college women (top figure, dashed lines), adolescent boys (bottom figure, solid lines), and college men (bottom figure, dashed lines). (Asterisks indicate figures rated most attractive by the opposite sex.)

College ratings adapted from A. E. Fallon & P. Rozin. (1985). Sex differences in perceptions of desirable body shape. *Journal of Abnormal Psychology, 94,* 102–105. From L. D. Cohn, N. E. Adler, C. E. Irwin, S. G. Millstein, S. M. Kegeles, & G. Stone. (1987). Body-figure preferences in male and female adolescents. *Journal of Abnormal Psychology, 96,* 278, Figure 1. Figures originally printed in "Use of the Danish Adoption Register for the Study of Obesity and Thinness" by A. J. Stunkard, T. Sorensen, and F. Schulsinger, 1983, in *The Genetics of Neurological and Psychiatric Disorders* (pp. 115–120). New York: Raven Press. Copyright 1983 by Raven Press. Reprinted by permission.

related with levels of eating disturbance (Fabian & Thompson, 1989; Grant & Fodor, 1986; Gross & Rosen, 1988), whereas, perceptual indices show little relationship (Fabian & Thompson). In a multiple regression study, Gross and Rosen (1988) found that body image dissatisfaction accounted for almost 21% of the total variance in global eating dysfunction in females.

Recently, Attie and Brooks-Gunn (1989) completed the first longitudinal study on the ability of certain variables, including appearance evaluation, to predict the development of eating disturbance. Subjects were measured two years apart (mean age of 13.93 years at first testing). At the first measurement, a poorer body image was significantly associated with greater eating disturbance. It was also found that Time 1 body image scores significantly predicted Time 2 levels of eating disturbance, while other variables such as general psychopathology, family relationships, and physical maturation were insignificant predictors.

Finally, in the first study to use causal modeling procedures to indicate the possible direction of the correlation between subjective body image dysfunction and eating disturbance (does body image dysfunction cause eating disturbance or vice versa?), Richards, Thompson, and Coovert (1990) evaluated 210 adolescents (ages 10–15) on multiple measures of body image, eating disturbance, and other variables (discussed further in the next chapter). Among other findings, Richards et al. (1990) found that poorer body image was causally related to greater eating disturbance. Interestingly, teasing history was also causally connected to body image disturbance (this finding is discussed at some length in the next chapter on theories of body image disturbance).

Other variables have also been associated with body image disturbance in adolescence. For instance, Lerner, Orlos, and Knapp (1976) had male and female adolescents rate 24 body characteristics in terms of how physically attractive they thought the parts were and how physically effective they thought the parts to be. Subjects also completed a self-concept scale. For females, the relationship between attractiveness and overall self-concept was higher than the connection between effectiveness and self-concept. The converse of these results was found with the male subjects.

Fabian and Thompson (1989) found that body satisfaction was highly correlated with overall self-esteem, teasing history, and depression level, in pre- and postmenarcheal females. However, these same researchers found that size overestimation was correlated with only one measure— the effect of teasing (subjects rated how severely the effects of teasing had been on them)—and this result was obtained only for the postmenarcheal subjects.

Research with adolescents has not been as extensive as that with adults; however, as the above discussion of longitudinal and causal modeling research indicates, this area has been characterized by a high quality of research. Notably absent in the great majority of these studies is work with males. In addition, the age range of subjects has been quite broad, ranging from 10–18 years of age in some investigations. In many cases, a specific breakdown of data by age is lacking. Also, the literature has notably neglected subjects below the age of 10. Future research should take these issues into consideration.

BALLET DANCERS
AND ATHLETES

In recent years, researchers have begun to evaluate body image disturbance in individuals thought to be at risk for the development of an eating disorder. Thus, various athletic forms, including running, wrestling, gymnastics, swimming, and ballet dance, have received empirical attention. This research is at a very young stage; the majority of research available is descriptive in form, therefore little evidence exists on the associated features of body image disturbance in these populations.

Ballet Dancers

Ballet dancers must meet very rigid requirements of weight and body shape. The ideal body for such an endeavor is one that is long and lean. Interestingly, very few studies have investigated body image disturbance in dancers, although various authors have noted that this group is at a high risk for the development of eating disorders (Hamilton, Brooks-Gunn, & Warren, 1985; Hamilton, Brooks-Gunn, Warren, & Hamilton, 1988). Garner, Garfinkel, Rockert, and Olmsted (1987) found that 25.7% of a sample of 35 ballet students had anorexia nervosa and 14.2% had bulimia nervosa. In this study, the authors tested the subjects longitudinally, in an attempt to find out what variables might predict the development of eating disturbance. They found that body dissatisfaction, along with a drive for thinness (a measure of eating disturbance) were the only two measures to predict the development of later eating problems.

Brooks-Gunn and Warren (1985) evaluated the effect of maturational timing on dance students' body satisfaction levels. Based on findings that late-maturing girls (age of menarche occurs after 14) are leaner and have lower levels of body fat than early or on-time maturers, they hypothesized that the former group would have less body image disturbance. (The role of maturational timing is fully discussed in the next chapter as a causative factor for body image disturbance.) These findings were confirmed—late maturers had less body image disturbance and also lower levels of perfectionism, bulimia, and general psychopathology.

Gargiulo, Brooks-Gunn, Attie, and Warren (1987) evaluated dancers and nondancers who were further broken down into different levels of pubertal development. They found that dancers had a poorer body image than nondancers, but only if the dancers also had accompanying breast development.

Only one study has evaluated body size estimation in dancers. Unfortunately, Meerman (1983) studied anorexics and a combined sample of ballet dancers and gymnasts (analyses were not computed separately for the groups). Both samples overestimated their body sizes and the anorexics overestimated to a larger degree on only 3 of 12 body sites.

In the most recent investigation to evaluate dancers, Brooks-Gunn, Burrow, and Warren (1988) compared this group to swimmers, figure skaters, and controls. In general, the dancers were more eating disturbed than any of the other three groups and also wanted to weigh less. Unfortunately, there was no formal measure of body image disturbance included in this study.

Athletes

Individuals who engage in repetitive exercise behavior may perform these activities for a variety of reasons. At the competitive level, reaching a certain level of performance is desirable and may necessitate the achievement of a certain body weight (wrestling, gymnastics, etc.) or body size (weightlifters). However, for the great majority of individuals who engage in exercise activities, the goal is some type of health maintenance or enhancement, recreational outlet, and/or the accomplishment of a certain appearance (Silberstein et al., 1988). With this latter issue in mind, it is apparent that many individuals use exercise as a weight-loss strategy or a means of reshaping the body's physique.

In recent years, researchers have begun to examine the association between exercise activity and eating disorders. The investigation of body image disturbance among exercisers has been an outgrowth of this body of research. The first study to empirically relate exercise activity and eating disturbance was conducted by Yates, Leehey, and Shisslak (1983) who put forth the hypothesis that "obligatory runners" (i.e., those who would not stop exercising even when injured) were psychologically similar to anorexics. They noted the following similarities in personality characteristics: suppression of anger, high self-expectations, tolerance of physical discomfort, and perfectionism. This study was widely criticized on methodological grounds and recent work suggests that runners do not exhibit nearly the psychopathology of eating-disordered subjects (Blumenthal, O'Toole, & Chang, 1984; Owens & Slade, 1987).

Research does indicate the possible presence of eating disturbance that may be problematic in athletic populations. Enns, Drewnowski, and Grinker (1987) evaluated wrestlers, swimmers, and cross-country skiers and found the wrestling subjects to have higher levels of eating disturbance. The authors concluded that "concern with weight may represent precursors for eating disorders associated with some forms of rigorous athletic training" (p. 63). The results may have represented the different athletic requirements for the groups—wrestlers are often required to meet exacting standards of weight (in many cases, engaging in hazardous weight-loss procedures to make weight for a certain match), whereas, skiers and swimmers have less of a requirement.

Pasman and Thompson (1988) evaluated male and female runners, weightlifters, and controls and found that both exercising groups had greater eating disturbance than normals, but did not differ from one another. However, a direct comparison of high-intensity male runners with female bulimia nervosa patients indicates that the eating-disordered individuals were more disturbed on all measures of eating disturbance (Nudelman, Rosen, & Leitenberg, 1988).

The assessment of eating disturbance and body image dysfunction in runners was the goal behind a recent national survey conducted by some of the most prominent researchers in this field (Brownell, Rodin, & Wilmore, 1988). Over 4,500 male and female runners were surveyed and 48% of the women and 24% of the men stated that they were preoccupied with the desire to be thinner. Almost identical numbers (48% and 21% respectively) noted that they were terrified of the prospect of gaining weight. Female respondents also noted that they often engaged in extreme behaviors to control their weight, such as self-induced vomiting, laxatives, and/or diuretics use. Twenty-six percent of the females reported the use of these procedures, whereas, only 4% of the men responded affirmatively. Over half (57%) of the females and 37% of the males reported that they were dissatisfied with their current body size and shape. It should be cautioned that this type of survey is always subject to bias because the more disturbed runners may have answered the survey in greater numbers than asymptomatic individuals.

The specific laboratory investigation of body image in these populations has also yielded important findings, primarily in the area of size estimation accuracy. For example, male runners have been found to overestimate body sizes to a greater extent than controls (Wheeler, Conger, Wall, Belcastro, & Cumming, 1986). High-mileage runners (over 40 miles per week) in the Wheeler et al. (1986) study were found to overestimate to a larger degree than low-mileage subjects (20–39 miles per week). Knight, Schocken, Powers, Feld, and Smith (1987), however, found that male and female runners underestimated the size of the waist and generally were more accurate than anorexics. Enns et al. (1987) did not find differences between wrestlers, swimmers, and cross-country skiers in degree of overestimation. In fact, each group was very accurate in its estimates (unfortunately, no control group was available for comparison). Enns et al. noted that a subsample of wrestlers who scored high on the eating disturbance measures, however, did display higher levels of overestimation.

Owens and Slade (1987) directly compared anorexics and long-distance runners on levels of perfectionism and body dissatisfaction. They found that the groups were similar on levels of perfectionism, but the runners' dissatisfaction scores resembled those of normal controls. They concluded that there were "superficial similarities" between runners and anorexics, but the "runners did not appear to suffer as a result" (p. 771).

Finally, two recent studies investigated both subjective and perceptual aspects of body image disturbance. Nudelman et al. (1988) compared male runners to female bulimics and found that there was no difference in their levels of overestimation (bulimics did, however, overestimate to a greater degree than a male control group, whereas, the male runners and controls were equivalent). On a subjective measure of satisfaction, however, bulimics scored lower than the runners and controls, who did not differ from one another. Pasman and Thompson (1988) evaluated runners, weightlifters, and sedentary controls. There were 30 subjects in each group, equally proportioned by gender. The results indicated that weightlifters were more accurate estimators of body size than runners and controls—this was true for both males and females. In addition, weightlifters of both genders were equally satisfied with their bodies. However, female runners and controls were significantly more dissatisfied with their bodies than male runners and controls. For a physical appearance evaluation measure, female runners had a poorer image of themselves than male runners. There were no differences between any of the other groups on this measure. Figure 2.5 contains the body satisfaction scores for the subjects studied by Pasman and Thompson.

Although research in this area is scarce, it appears that females (especially runners) may have a greater level of disturbance than males. In addition, wrestlers may be at a higher risk for the development of eating disturbance, and weightlifters appear to have less body image dysfunction than other groups. Interestingly, male runners and controls showed the expected greater satisfaction with body image than females, while weightlifters of both genders were equivalent. It would be worthwhile to further explore the role of weightlifting in equalizing body satisfaction across gender. In addition, weightlifters of both genders were extremely accurate in the estimation of body sizes, a finding

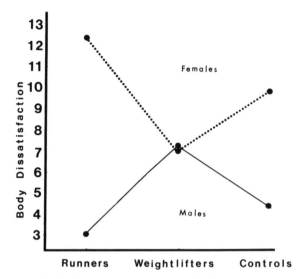

FIGURE 2.5. Mean body dissatisfaction scores for male and female runners, weight-lifters, and sedentary controls (age range: 18–60).

Adapted from data contained in L. Pasman & J. K. Thompson. (1988). Body image and eating distur-bance in obligatory runners, obligatory weightlifters, and sedentary individuals. *International Journal of Eating Disorders, 7*, 759–770.

that deserves replication. Pasman and Thompson (1988) hypothesized that the greater exposure to mirrors by the weightlifters (thus, percep-tual feedback) might account for this greater accuracy.

Notably lacking in research on athletes and dancers are systematic studies designed to look at the associated features of body image dis-turbance. In addition, greater care should be taken in defining subject groups. In some studies, samples were composed of college athletes while others contained recreational athletes. Males and females need to be evaluated in the same studies, and this has seldom taken place. Athletes should also be categorized based on their motivation for ex-ercise (Silberstein et al., 1988). Individuals who engage in physical ac-tivities for the purpose of weight and shape management may system-atically differ from those who exercise for health reasons or because of some underlying eating disorder or obsessive-compulsive personality disorder. With this in mind, it would appear important to eliminate clinically diagnosed anorexics or bulimics from samples because the in-clusion of these individuals may bias the data, causing researchers to conclude that athletes may be generally disturbed on certain features. Removal of data collected on eating-disordered individuals who also exercise might refine our analysis of body image in athletic popula-tions. Finally, researchers have also stated the importance of distinguishing the casual exerciser from the addicted athlete or "obligatory" exerciser (Thompson & Blanton, 1987). The obligatory athlete is characterized by an inability to stop exercising, even if situational factors such as injury or illness indicate that cessation is advisable. Pasman and Thompson (1988) recently developed the Oligatory Exercise Scale to aid in the designation of these particular types of athletes (see Appendix A).

OBESE INDIVIDUALS

At first glance, it might appear that body image research with the obese would prove useless. From a subjective analysis, one might assume that all obese persons are dissatisfied with their body size and appearance. From a size estimation view, is it possible that they overestimate their already enlarged size? However, these are important issues. For instance, if obese subjects lose weight does their body image disturbance—satisfaction and/or size estimation accuracy—also change? Are body image indices correlated with treatment progress? Finally, from a developmental perspective, does age of onset of obesity (juvenile vs. adult) have any relationship to size estimation?

The above questions have led researchers to conduct several investigations on body image in the obese. In general, research strongly supports the common sense observation that overweight individuals are unhappy with the way they look (Allon, 1982; Whitaker et al., 1989). With regard to the effect of weight loss on body size perception, the findings are mixed. Glucksman and Hirsch (1969) evaluated six obese and four nonobese individuals who were hospitalized for weight reduction. Size estimates were obtained once weekly for eight months— during this time they lost an average of 87 pounds. Nonobese controls were tested once weekly for six consecutive weeks. As they lost weight, the level of overestimation increased for the obese, but there was no change in estimates for the nonobese.

Stunkard and Burt (1967) first noted that time of onset of obesity was a factor in adult body image dissatisfaction. They evaluated obese adults who had been obese as children and adolescents with those whose obesity had its onset in adulthood. Of the 23 subjects whose onset was juvenile, 14 had severe body image disturbance, whereas, none of the 40 adult onset obesity subjects reported severe disturbance—in fact, 30 reported experiencing no discomfort regarding appearance.

Grinker (1973) evaluated the effect of weight loss on body size perception in individuals who had been obese since childhood and those who had adult-onset obesity. With increasing weight loss the latter group underestimated their body sizes while the juvenile-onset group came to overestimate. Adult-onset subjects were also more accurate when allowed to observe themselves in a mirror while the opposite was the case for the juvenile-onset group. Chwast (1978; cited in Fisher, 1986), in a more extensive analysis of the effects of weight loss on size estimation, utilized larger sample sizes and improved methodology. Obese individuals, divided into early onset and adult onset, were compared to a control group of normal women. All groups were tested at pre- and posttreatment when the obese had lost 23% of their weight. The obese subjects became significantly more accurate in their body size judgments following weight loss—time of onset of obesity had little impact. Finally, in a sample of adolescent males, Speaker, Schultz, Grinker, and Stern (1983) found that subjects were accurate prior to weight reduction and underestimated sizes following weight loss (average of 29.3 lb).

A few studies have directly compared the size perception accuracy of obese individuals to other subject populations. For example, Garner, Garfinkel, Stancer, & Moldofsky (1976) compared individuals with juvenile-onset obesity, anorexics, "thin normals," psychiatric controls, and normals. On one size estimation measure (whole-image adjustment) the obese did not differ from the anorexics, but did overestimate more than the other three groups. Estimates were largely equivalent across groups when a single site estimation procedure was utilized. Thompson et al. (1986) found that bulimic and nonbulimic obese subjects overestimated to the same degree as anorexics and previously anorexic bulimics. However, a sample of normal-weight bulimics, without a history of anorexia, overestimated body sizes to a larger degree than both obese groups.

Fisher (1986) recently reviewed the literature in this area and concluded that the type of size estimation accuracy procedure that researchers utilize may have an effect on subjects' level of overestimation. Specifically, studies that utilized a site estimation procedure (which requires that subjects estimate the sizes of certain body sites) failed to find an obese-normal difference in level of overestimation. However, studies that use a whole-body adjustment procedure (which requires that subjects adjust the image of their entire body) have shown that the obese overestimate to a larger degree than do controls. He also concluded that the juvenile- vs. adult-onset distinction made little difference in size overestimation in the majority of well-controlled studies. In addition, Fisher (1986) noted that research had not documented a positive correlation between level of obesity and level of perceptual inaccuracy. Finally, individuals who were currently of normal weight, with a history of obesity (formerly obese) were no different than those of normal weight with no history of obesity.

Two studies not included in the Fisher (1986) review also add to our understanding of size estimation in the obese. Collins, McCabe, and Sutton (1983) took pre- and posttreatment measures of size mation (using a whole-body image adjustment procedure) on 68 won who underwent treatment for obesity. These authors found that drop- outs from the program overestimated significantly more (26%) than did those individuals who completed treatment (19%). In addition, when subjects were dichotomized based on mean weight, it was found that the heaviest group overestimated more than did the moderately obese subjects (24% vs. 19%). Subjects who completed treatment reduced their overestimation from 19% to 8.8%. Unfortunately, in this study, sub- jects were not subdivided by onset of obesity (early vs. late), and con- trol subjects were not included as a comparison sample.

Gardner, Morrell, Urrutia, and Espinoza (in press) measured the size estimation accuracy (again, using a whole-body adjustment method) in 13 subjects who had already lost weight (10 from a gastric bypass pro- cedure). These estimates were compared to those of a normal-weight control group. The results indicated that the obese overestimated less (4.8%) than the controls (18.6%). Unfortunately, no pre-weight-loss data was available and, again, subjects were not divided by onset of obesity.

Relatively little work has been done on the associated features of body image disturbance in the obese. Mendelson and White (1982) looked at the relationship between self-esteem and body satisfaction in nor- mal-weight and obese children (15 boys and 21 girls). Correlations were very high and roughly equivalent for the obese and the nonobese. However, the number of subjects in their study was very small and these correlations are quite suspect.

Future research in this area should clearly specify subjects' time of obesity onset as a factor in the assessment of the effect of weight change on body image indices. In addition, subjective measures are sorely lacking in this literature and should be included—clinically, it is pos- sible that subjects' satisfaction with weight loss may not parallel their perceptual changes. The relationship between body image indices and other measures of psychological functioning has also received limited investigation in the obese. Finally, many studies have not evaluated the effects of gender or age—two variables that may moderate any ob- served findings.

ANOREXIA NERVOSA AND BULIMIA NERVOSA

As discussed in Chapter 1, the initial interest in the physical appear- ance aspect of body image was engendered by its recognition as a key factor in the pathogenesis of anorexia nervosa. The failure of anorexics to report that they were aware of their emaciated state led to a focus on the size estimation component of body image in this population. The measurement of size overestimation in anorexia and its correlates created a phenomenal interest in researchers, who developed a wide variety of procedures for assessing this particular aspect of body image (Cash & Brown, 1987; Garner, 1981; Garner & Garfinkel, 1981; Garner, Garfinkel, & Bonato, 1987; Slade, 1985; Thompson et al., 1990; this is discussed at length in Chapter 4). Interestingly, the measurement of subjective aspects of body image has received far less attention than the perceptual component. In fact, there now exist more studies with asymptomatic subjects' subjective disturbance (see earlier discussion in this chapter) than with the subjective dysfunction of individuals with anorexia nervosa or bulimia nervosa. Therefore, in this section, the primary focus is on the perceptual size overestimation studies for anorexia nervosa and, to a lesser extent, bulimia nervosa. It should be noted that, unless specifically mentioned, all the succeeding studies deal with female populations.

Extent of Disturbance

As noted earlier in this chapter, it is now well documented that size overestimation is not limited to the eating disordered populations (Fabian & Thompson, 1989; Pasman & Thompson, 1988; Thompson & Thompson, 1986). Many researchers have failed to detect a difference between asymptomatic subjects and eating-disordered individuals (Cash & Brown, 1987). However, in the only review to summarize results across a wide variety of subjects, Slade (1985) found a larger degree of overestimation in anorexics as compared to controls. Slade separately evaluated size overestimation for different estimation procedures (site vs. whole-body techniques). For the site estimation techniques, he found an average of 24% overestimation for anorexics and 16% for controls. For the whole-body adjustment procedures, anorexics averaged 1.72% overestimation while the controls underestimated by 3.27%.

More-recent investigations have begun to include an analysis of bulimics' level of size overestimation. Willmuth, Leitenberg, Rosen, Fondacaro, and Gross (1985) found that bulimics overestimated to a larger degree than did controls; however, Counts and Adams (1985) found no differences between bulimics, previously obese subjects, normal-weight dieters, and controls. Touyz, Beumont, Collins, and Cowie (1985) directly compared samples of anorexics and bulimics for size estimation. Anorexics overestimated to a lesser degree than bulimics. Thompson et al. (1986) found that a sample of normal-weight bulimics, without a previous history of anorexia, had higher levels of inaccuracy than did controls, obese individuals, or anorexics. Lindholm and Wilson (1988) compared bulimics to two control groups—one reported a good deal of "restrained" eating or dieting behavior, while the other did not self-report "restrained" eating patterns. In general, the bulimics and re-strained controls overestimated to a larger degree than nonrestrained controls, but there were few differences between bulimics and re-strained controls. Willmuth, Leitenberg, Rosen, and Cado (1988) found that purging bulimics overestimated body size to a greater degree than nonpurging bulimics or controls.

Because of the often small differences in absolute levels of overesti-mation between clinical and control subjects, some researchers have begun to investigate other aspects of the perceptual component. For instance, several researchers have noted that anorexics may be more variable in their perception of body sizes, that is, show more extremes of overestimation and underestimation (Garner et al., 1976; Pierloot & Houben, 1978; Touyz, Beumont, Collins, McCabe, & Jupp, 1984). In the most recent analysis of this question, anorexics, bulimics, obese individuals, and controls were tested for size estimation accuracy, with a focus on the variability of responses across groups (Collins, Beumont, Touyz, Krass, Thompson, & Phillips, 1987b). The obese and bulimic subjects showed the greatest variability of overestimation, followed by the anorexics and controls.

One factor that may contribute to the variability of overestimation found in some studies with clinical samples is the effect of instructions. As noted earlier, Thompson and Dolce (1989), in a sample of normal college women, found that estimates based on how subjects "felt" about their bodies produced larger indices of overestimation than estimates based on a rational judgment of size. Huon and Brown (1986) found essentially similar findings in samples of eating-disordered individuals. For both bulimic and anorexic samples, levels of overestimation were higher when subjects rated based on affective instructions.

As noted by Garner, Garfinkel, and Bonato (1987), "there have been surprisingly few studies of body dissatisfaction in anorexia nervosa and bulimia nervosa despite the logical connection between this construct and the dieting behavior typically associated with these disorders" (p. 126). Casper, Offer, and Ostrov (1981) found that late adolescent an-orexics had a greater degree of dissatisfaction than a normal control group. Counts and Adams (1985), using the perceived-ideal discrep-ancy measure of satisfaction, found no differences between bulimics, dieters (previously overweight, but currently not obese), and "re-strained controls." Each of these three groups, however, had greater dissatisfaction than a normal control group. Lindholm and Wilson (1988) replicated the Counts and Adams (1985) study—bulimics and re-strained controls had greater discrepancies than "unrestrained" con-trols.

Three recent studies have evaluated the subjective aspects of body image disturbance in bulimic samples subdivided into smaller groups. For example, Post and Crowther (1987) found that purging bulimic adolescents had a more negative perception of their current weight and attached a greater importance to the achievement of ideal body weight than did nonpurging subjects. They concluded that "these findings implicate body image disturbance as related to the more severe behavioral manifestations of this disorder" (p. 757). In a replication of these findings with adults, Davis, Williamson, Goreczny, and Bennett (in press), found that nonpurging bulimics were less disturbed than purging bulimics. Thompson (1988a) found that underweight purgers had less body dissatisfaction than did normal-weight purgers (with and without a history of being underweight). His explanation was that the underweight bulimics' "body weight *is* lower and, maybe, more acceptable to them" (p. 189).

Correlates of Disturbance

Even though evidence continues to question the relative quantity of overestimation in eating-disordered samples and whether this amount is higher than in asymptomatic controls, researchers have shown quite clearly that the overestimation is related strongly to clinically significant variables. In addition, some research has addressed the correspondence between subjective disturbance and other clinically relevant variables. In the seminal investigation in this area, Slade and Russell (1973) found that subjects' level of overestimation decreased as they gained weight, and the degree of overestimation was strongly related to progress following hospitalization—subjects whose size overestimation was not attenuated by weight gain were more likely to relapse. The connection between high levels of inaccuracy and relapse was replicated by other authors (Cash & Brown, 1987). Recently, Touyz, Beumont, and Collins (1988) compared anorexic overestimators to underestimators during a five-week period of weight gain. Interestingly, there was no difference between the two groups in the amount of weight gained; however, follow-up data were not reported.

Freeman and colleagues have also noted the predictive ability of body image disturbance for indentifying individuals at risk for relapse in bulimia nervosa (Freeman, Beach, Davis, & Solyom, 1985). These researchers used a discrepancy measure (estimated minus ideal) and a size overestimation index, along with several other variables in a regression equation to determine which factor was most important in predicting relapse. They found that the dissatisfaction measure (discrepancy) and frequency of initial bingeing were the only two significant predictors; however, an analysis of the regression weights indicated that dissatisfaction with body image at the conclusion of treatment was "by far the most potent predictor of relapse in the patients studied" (p. 351).

In anorexic patients, level of absolute overestimation has been found to be highly connected to low self-esteem, low ego strength, external locus of control and neuroticism (see Garner & Garfinkel, 1981; Garner, Garfinkel, & Bonato, 1987). Garner and Garfinkel dichotomized anorexics by degree of overestimation into marked overestimators vs. those who underestimated or only slightly overestimated. They found that those who markedly overestimated had higher levels of anxiety, physical anhedonia, eating pathology, and depression. In a sample of adolescent anorexics, Strober (1981) used a canonical correlational procedure to evaluate the relationship between body image and personality. Two dimensions emerged from this methodology. The first dimension found that size overestimation and subjective disturbance were associated with somatization, anxiety, and atypical thinking. In the second canonical variate, size overestimation was related to introversion and depression, but subjective disturbance was connected with somatization and atypical thinking. He concluded that "different measures of body image disturbance are associated with different personality characteristics" (p. 323).

Therefore, it appears that level of overestimation, even though research suggests that it is not specific to anorexia nervosa or bulimia nervosa, may be importantly related to other clinical phenomena for these disorders. Garner, Garfinkel, and Bonato (1987) also maintain that different forms of body image disturbance may characterize eating-disordered patients and that "these may selectively operate for some patients and not for others" (p. 125). For instance, they suggest that size misperception may not be relevant for some patients, that instead they may desire a certain shape that is unreasonable or disparage a certain body site (along the lines of a Body Dysmorphic Disorder, discussed in Chapter 6). They note that research should focus on the clarification of specific types of body image disturbance for different subgroups of eating-disordered patients. In effect, the issue is one of a multifaceted assessment procedure, designed to determine the idiosyncratic type of body image dysfunction for a specific patient. This concept of an idiographic approach is revisited in the following chapters on assessment and treatment.

Current Trends

Current research in this area has focused on dichotomizing nonclinical subjects into eating-disturbed and asymptomatic groups based on questionnaire measures of eating disturbance. For example, Zellner, Harner, and Adler (1989) compared women who scored in the anorexic

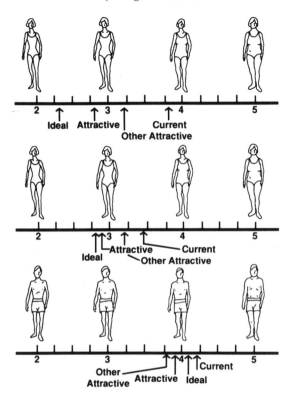

FIGURE 2.6. Mean ratings of eating-disturbed women (A), non-eating-disturbed women (B), and men for ideal figure, current figure, figure most attractive to the opposite sex, and figure rated most attractive by the opposite sex (labeled "Other Attractive"). (Sample: college students, ages unspecified).

From D. A. Zellner, D. E. Harner & R. L. Adler. (1989). Effects of eating abnormalities and gender perceptions of desirable body shape. *Journal of Abnormal Psychology, 98,* 95, Figure 1. Figures originally printed in "Use of the Danish Adoption Register for the Study of Obesity and Thinness" by A. J. Stunkard, T. Sorensen, and F. Schulsinger, 1983, in *The Genetics of Neurological and Psychiatric Disorders* (pp. 115–120). New York: Raven Press. Copyright 1983 by Raven Press. Reprinted by permission.

range on the Eating Attitudes Test with low scorers. Subjects, using the Figure-Rating Scales, picked their current figure, ideal figure, and the figure they thought was most attractive to the opposite sex. They found that subjects in both groups rated their current figure as larger than the figure they thought would be most attractive to the opposite sex. In addition both groups rated their current figure as larger than their ideal figure. However, the eating-disordered subjects rated their ideal as significantly smaller than the figure they thought was most attractive to the opposite sex, whereas there was no difference between the two ratings for the subjects with a low level of eating disturbance. These results are contained in Figure 2.6.

These findings were recently replicated by Thompson (1990) who dichotomized subjects according to a measure of bulimic behavior (Bulimia Test). The results indicated that (a) eating-disturbed subjects' rating of how they felt was larger than asymptomatic subjects' rating, (b) eating-disturbed subjects' rating of how they thought they looked was also larger than nondisturbed subjects' figure selection, (c) the disturbed group rated how others saw them as larger than the asymptomatic subjects, and (d) there were no differences between groups on ratings of ideal size and the size most attractive to men. Eating-disturbed subjects also scored higher on a general measure of physical appearance satisfaction and teasing history. The results of this study are contained in Figure 2.7.

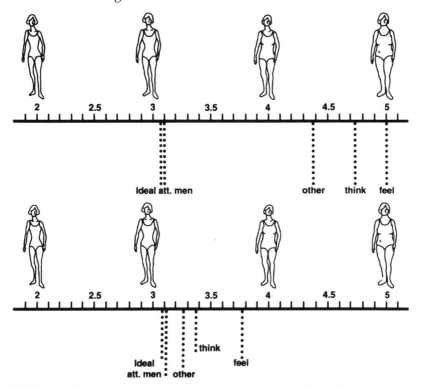

FIGURE 2.7. Mean ratings for eating-disturbed and non-eating-disturbed women for ideal figure, how they *think* they look, how they *feel* they look, how they appear to others, and the figure most attractive to men.

From J. K. Thompson. (1990). *Body shape preferences: Effects of instructional protocol and level of eating disturbance*. Unpublished manuscript. Figures originally printed in "Use of the Danish Adoption Register for the Study of Obesity and Thinness" by A. J. Stunkard, T. Sorensen, and F. Schulsinger, 1983, in *The Genetics of Neurological and Psychiatric Disorders* (pp. 115–120). New York: Raven Press. Copyright 1983 by Raven Press. Reprinted by permission.

Brown, Cash, and Lewis (1989) identified a sample of 114 adolescent female binge-purgers from a larger nationwide survey of 1,262 females aged 15–19 years old. A control group was composed of individuals who were matched with the clinical subjects on age, weight, and height. These two groups were compared on a variety of body image indices. As expected, the binge-purgers had a poorer appearance evaluation, greater dissatisfaction with body sites, and higher disturbance on a number of weight-related measures.

In all likelihood, future research with eating-disordered populations will focus on many different aspects of body image disturbance (Rosen, 1990). The assessment of body image in eating-disturbed subjects, selected from larger surveys of "normal" populations, will also increase in the future. This research has the advantage of eliminating patient status as a possible confound when simply comparing eating-disorder patients to nonpatient controls. Future research should also focus on categorizing eating-disordered populations into meaningful subgroups that may differ on body image disturbance. In this regard, the purging vs. nonpurging dimension would appear to be very important (Davis et al., in press; Post & Crowther, 1987; Willmuth et al., 1988).

SUMMARY

This chapter has presented a broad overview of the extent and correlates of body image disturbance in various populations. It is apparent that significant levels of discomfort are extant and that this dysfunction is associated with many different clinically relevant variables, including, eating disturbance, depression, lowered self-esteem, and general psychological distress. It is also apparent that females suffer to a far greater degree than males, whether they are adolescents or adults. However, this conclusion must be accompanied by a caveat—research with noncollege students is almost nonexistent. It is very possible, even likely, that males in their late twenties and early thirties, especially in high-profile settings, will report moderately high levels of body image concerns. Research with adolescents who are under the age of 10 is also meager and the investigation of body image concerns in the elderly is also indicated (Stelnicki & Thompson, 1989). The next chapter extends our understanding of body image disturbance and its correlates by examining possible causal mechanisms for the development of body image and its dysfunction.

Chapter 3

Theories of Body
Image Disturbance

This chapter provides a brief overview of theories of body image disturbance. First, an overview of cortical components of body image is offered, followed by a discussion of developmental issues, primarily focusing on the important role of puberty for females' body image development. A sociocultural explanation of body image disturbance is then analyzed; this particular viewpoint encompasses the bulk of the chapter. Three fairly concise approaches—self-ideal discrepancy theory, adaptive failure theory, and perceptual artifact theory—are then discussed. Finally, models of laboratory-induced dysfunction are reviewed.

CORTICAL ASPECTS
OF DISTURBANCE

The first writings on body image were done by individuals in neurology (McCrea et al., 1982; Shontz, 1974); however, their conceptions were much different than the physical appearance-related construct discussed so far in this book. The initial descriptions dealt with instances of phantom limb phenomena—the illusory feeling of the presence of a limb that had been previously amputated from the body. Another cortical component of body image involves the inability to distinguish the left side of the body from the right (anosognosia) or the complete denial of the existence of parts of the body (neglect). These phenomena appear to be most commonly associated with brain damage to the parietal regions (usually right side) of the brain.

Very little work has been conducted on cortical components of the physical appearance components of body image. In the only study to directly relate neuropsychological function to some component of body image, Thompson and Spana (1990) hypothesized that size overestimation, because it is a largely visuospatial ability, might positively relate to a general visuospatial dysfunction, as measured with traditional neuropsychological instruments. In this study, college students were administered the Benton Visual Retention Test, which consists of the presentation of 10 geometric designs, for a period of 10 seconds. Following each presentation, subjects are asked to draw the design from memory. Performance is gauged in terms of total number of errors. Subjects were also measured for size estimation accuracy. The results indicated that there were significant correlations between level of overestimation and errors in visual memory for the hip and thigh body sites.

Several researchers have addressed the relationship between neuropsychological deficits and level of eating disturbance (Kowalski, 1986; Strauss & Ryan, 1988), and this is an important area of research. However, this approach only indirectly addresses the issue of body image and cortical functioning. Future research, along the lines of Thompson and Spana (1990), should investigate the specific connection between neuropsychological indices designed to measure some aspect of visuospatial functioning and size estimation accuracy.

DEVELOPMENTAL FACTORS

A good deal of work has focused on the important transitional role that puberty plays in the development of body image, especially in females. The time of pubertal developmental lasts several years and is associated with multiple physical and psychological changes for the adolescent girl. Normally the epoch of menarche is chosen as a critical variable for research purposes, because of its association with self-image, body image, peer relationships, and parental relationships (Brooks-Gunn & Warren, 1985, 1988; Tobin-Richards et al., 1983).

For example, Koff, Rierdan, and Silverstone (1978) found that postmenarcheal girls indicated greater satisfaction with body parts than premenarcheal girls; however, Gargiulo et al. (1987) found no relationship between menarcheal status and body satisfaction. Fabian and Thompson (1989) compared premenarcheal and postmenarcheal girls on perceptual and subjective measures of body image. Interestingly, there were few differences between groups; however, the premenarcheal girls overestimated their thighs to a greater degree than the postmenarcheal girls. When the associations between body image indices and other variables were examined, however, some important differences emerged. For postmenarcheal girls, size overestimation at each body site (cheeks, waist, hips, thighs) was positively correlated with teasing history. This was not true for the premenarcheal girls. In addition, for both groups, teasing history was positively associated with body dissatisfaction. Table 3.1 contains the findings from Fabian and Thompson.

Other work in this area has focused on the association between time of menarche onset and body image. Generally the results suggest that girls who mature later (experience menarche after the age of 14) have a more positive body image than those who have their first menstrual period on time or early (before the age of 11). For instance, Brooks-Gunn and Warren (1985) found that on-time girls had greater body dissatisfaction, body fat, overall weight, and eating disturbance than late maturers. Duncan, Ritter, Dornbusch, Gross, and Carlsmith (1985) found that more early maturers wanted to be thinner (69%) than on-time girls (53%) or late-maturers (27%). None of the early maturers wanted to be heavier while 22% of the late maturers wanted to gain weight. These findings have also been replicated when girls' self-perception of maturational status has been used as the defining index (Tobin-Richards et al., 1983) although Gargiulo et al. (1987) found that girls who rated themselves as on time had marginally significant higher satisfaction than those who perceived themselves to be early or late. Bruch (1981) thought that early maturation was a risk factor for anorexia. Striegel-Moore, Silberstein, and Rodin (1986) also concluded that "maturing faster than her peers may place a girl at risk for bulimia as well" (p. 253).

Interestingly, early maturation appears to be associated with positive experiences for boys, since early maturers have been found to have a more positive body image and more confidence than late maturers (Clausen, 1975; Tobin-Richards et al., 1983). A biological difference at puberty may explain some of the gender differences. Girls' weight gain at puberty is primarily adipose tissue, whereas boys' weight gain is dominated by an increase in muscle and lean body tissue (Beller, 1977; Marino & King, 1980). Reinforcing this biological change is a congruent societal value for men—increased size and a muscular appearance. On the other hand, society values the opposite of the added fat deposition that is taking place for girls—a thin, svelte figure.

Another explanation for the negative effects for some girls and not for others may lie in the increased weight gain and shape changes for early, and, possibly on-timers, when compared to their female peers who have yet to experience the effects of puberty. In fact, these changes may be permanent. Garn, LaVelle, Rosenberg, and Hawthorne (1986) found that adult early maturers were shorter than late maturers, but

Table 3.1. Intercorrelations among variables for premenarche and postmenarche adolescent females (ages 10–15)

						Premenarche						
Postmenarche	Ch	Wt	Hp	Th	GM	SE	BE	DE	ED	TF	TE	AG
Ch	—	.38**	.22	.17	.58	-.10	.08	.16	.07	.03	.09	-.16
Wt	.34**	—	.61**	.34**	.72**	-.05	.07	.05	-.05	-.24	.18	-.20
Hp	.40**	.78**	—	.64**	.82**	-.10	-.06	-.01	.02	.00	.12	-.04
Th	.48**	.62**	.65**	—	.78**	-.14	-.14	.07	.14	-.09	.16	-.17
GM	.65**	.86**	.87**	.82**	—	-.12	-.02	-.17	.04	-.06	.17	-.17
SE	.03	-.18	-.14	-.22	-.13	—	.62**	-.67**	-.59**	-.25*	-.33**	.28**
BE	.00	-.18	-.21	-.23	-.18	.47**	—	-.70**	-.69**	-.35**	-.46**	.14
DE	.00	.37**	.34**	.28**	.33**	-.56**	-.52**	—	.53**	.36**	.40**	-.16
ED	-.01	.19	.21	.17	.17	-.41**	.50**	.41**	—	.30*	.50**	-.37**
TF	.15	.08	.06	.00	.08	.06	-.25*	.06	-.10	—	.26	.06
TE	.27*	.27*	.26*	.32*	.33**	-.17	-.11	.30*	.39**	.20	—	.27*
AG	-.16	.05	-.05	-.02	-.05	-.09	.01	.06	-.08	-.07	-.12	—
MP	-.26*	-.09	-.17	-.15	-.18	-.03	.07	.08	.08	-.12	-.04	.67**

From L. J. Fabian & J. K. Thompson (1989). Body image and eating disturbance in young females. *International Journal of Eating Disorders, 8,* 69, Table 2. Copyright © 1989 by John Wiley and Sons. Reprinted by permission of John Wiley and Sons, Inc.

Note: Ch = cheeks, Wt = waist, Hp = hips, Th = thighs, GM = global mean, SE = self-esteem, BE = body esteem, DE = depression, ED = eating disturbance, TF = teasing frequency, TE = teasing effect, AG = age, MP = months postmenarche.

*p < .05.

**p < .01.

weighed 8.8 pounds more and had 30% more body fat. When Simmons, Blyth, and McKinney (1983) corrected for total body weight, the differences in body satisfaction between girls of different developmental timings disappeared.

To some degree, the negative findings for body image and timing may not extend to other aspects of adolescent functioning. For instance, Simmons et al. (1983) found that early-maturing girls had greater popularity among boys and Clausen (1975) found them to have greater self-confidence. However, there have also been other negative aspects tied to early maturation, including greater emotional distress, lower self-concepts, and less popularity among female peers (Peskin, 1973; Simmons et al., 1983). Although much work remains to be done in this area, maturational timing seems to be an important factor in adolescents' and adults' body image disturbance.

Teasing history has also recently been posited as a factor in the development of body image disturbance. Adult women who were teased about their appearance as children have been found to have less satisfaction with their bodies as adults than those who were not teased (Berscheid, Walster, & Bohrnstedt, 1973; Cash et al., 1986). Fabian and Thompson (1989) also found high correlations between dissatisfaction and teasing history. Recently, Richards et al. (1990), using causal modeling procedures, found that teasing was causally related to body dissatisfaction and general psychological dysfunction (depression, lowered self-esteem). Interestingly, these researchers found that the proposed causal connection from maturational status to teasing history and body image disturbance was not significant. However, the paths from actual weight (objective weight, compared to norms) to teasing history and body image disturbance were significant, indicating that greater weight caused an increase in teasing and poorer body image. Subjects' perceived weight (how they categorized their own weight) was also positively related to body image disturbance. Figure 3.1 contains these findings.

It is likely that the role of developmental variables such as menarche, maturational timing, and teasing history will receive added attention as mediators of body image disturbance in future years. Because investigators have recently created multiple ways of quantifying pubertal status (Brooks-Gunn & Warren, 1988) future research should not be limited by a single developmental milestone, such as menarche. In addition, until recently, there was no available measure of teasing history; however, Thompson, Fabian, and Moulton (1990) recently devised a psychometrically sound instrument to assess this construct (see Appendix B). Future research should also focus on the relationships

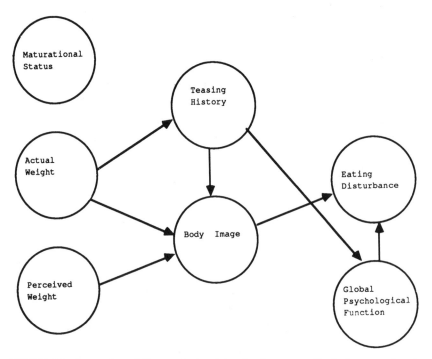

FIGURE 3.1. A causal modeling analysis of the development of body image and eating disturbance. Significant paths are noted with directional arrows (Sample: adolescent females: age range 10–15).

From K. J. Richards, J. K. Thompson, & M. Coovert (1990). *Development of body image and eating disturbance in adolescent females*. Unpublished manuscript.

between pubertal development, body image, and other significant variables, such as self-esteem, depression, and general psychological functioning.

SOCIOCULTURAL THEORIES

By far the most supported theoretical explanation for our society's large level of body image disturbance is the sociocultural approach. This model maintains that current societal standards for beauty inordinately emphasize the desirability of thinness. In many ways, the media have fostered the view that "thinness equals beauty." In addition, a wealth of research has indicated that our society negatively values the opposite of thinness—obesity (Allon, 1982; Hawkins & Clement, 1984; Rodin et al., 1985; Rothblum, Miller, & Garbutt, 1988). As succinctly captured by Striegel-Moore, Silberstein, and Rodin (1986) "the more a woman believes that 'what is fat is bad, what is thin is beautiful, and what is beautiful is good,' the more she will work toward thinness and be distressed about fatness" (p. 247). In addition, as Silberstein et al. (1987) note "From birth, females are indoctrinated with the message that they should be pretty—which in this sociohistorical moment means being thin" (p. 92). Hsu (1989) has indicated that the "more intensive pressure on women to be slim" (p. 393) may account for the larger prevalence of eating disorders in women.

Support for the sociocultural view comes from a variety of sources. First, research strongly suggests that society has changed its conception of the figure that women should aspire to in recent years. Garner, Garfinkel, Schwartz, and Thompson (1980) reviewed the weights of Miss America contestants since 1960 and used covariance procedures to negate the effects of changing heights and sizes of *Playboy* centerfolds. They found that the weights had decreased significantly over that time period. These same researchers also noted that the number of diet articles in major magazines had increased substantially during the same years. Figures 3.2 and 3.3 illustrate these changes over time.

Agras and Kirkley (1986) have also documented the changing nature of the most socially desirable body shape. They reviewed three women's magazines from 1900 to 1986 and devised an index of thinness. From a random selection of pictures from the magazines, they found that the ideal look had varied drastically over this century, from a larger figure to the thin look of the 1920s, back to a fuller figure, and finally

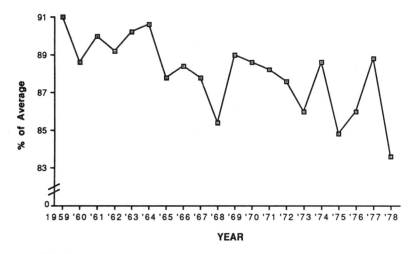

FIGURE 3.2. Changes in percent of average weight of *Playboy* centerfolds over 20 years.

Reprinted with permission of authors and publisher from: Garner, D. M., Garfinkel, P. E., Schwartz, D., and Thompson, M. Cultural expectations of thinness in women. *Psychological Reports*, 1980, 47, 485, Figure 1.

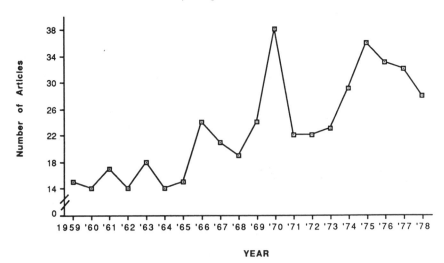

YEAR

FIGURE 3.3. Diet articles in six popular women's magazines over 20 years.

Reprinted with permission of authors and publisher from: Garner, D. M., Garfinkel, P. E., Schwartz, D., and Thompson, M. Cultural expectations of thinness in women. *Psychological Reports*, 1980, 47, 489, Figure 5.

to the thin shape of the present time. They also replicated the drastic increase in dieting articles that Garner et al. (1980) found in their research. Figure 3.4 illustrates the results of their survey.

Silverstein, Peterson, and Perdue (1986) created an index of curvaceousness and measured women who appeared in *Vogue* and *Ladies Home Journal*, beginning in 1901. Using millimeter rulers, they measured the bust, waist, and hips and developed a ratio between the measures (to control for the size of the photographs). Lower ratios reflected increasing slenderness, that is, a lack of curvaceousness. Figure 3.5 contains their findings.

In a second study, Silverstein, Perdue, Peterson, and Kelly (1986) examined 48 men's and women's magazines and catalogued the frequencies of articles and advertisements that dealt with dietary issues (shape, foods, changing figure). They found a female-male ratio of the frequency of occurrence of dietary issues of 159 to 13.

Authors have recently begun to examine the powerful effects of the mass media (Freedman, 1986). Lakoff and Scherr (1984) have specifically noted the influence of television and magazine mass media as problematic. They suggested that individuals in these milieus are seen as realistic representations of actual people, as opposed to painted figures and sculptures, which may be seen as artistic creations. The public may fail to realize that models in pictures and on screen may spend many hours on developing a certain look, including rigidly controlled

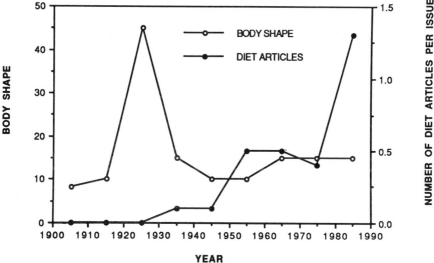

FIGURE 3.4. The body shape of women depicted in pictures and advertisements in three women's magazines from 1900 to 1985. Higher scores are associated with thinner body shapes.

From W. S. Agras & B. G. Kirkley (1986). Bulimia: Theories of etiology. In K. D. Brownell and J. P. Foreyt (Eds.), *Handbook of eating disorders: Physiology, psychology, and treatment of obesity, anorexia, and bulimia* (p. 370). New York: Basic Books. Copyright © 1986 by Basic Books. Reprinted by permission of Basic Books Inc., Publishers.

diet and exercise and professional makeup, whereas, the individual who has a regular job or is a student can afford no such indulgences. Unfortunately, we may fail to realize that the model's accomplishment may be completely unrealistic for the "common" person.

Striegel-Moore, Silberstein, and Rodin (1986) also note that the current fascination with fitness may have the effect of convincing us that "anyone who 'works out' can achieve the lean, healthy-looking ideal" (p. 257). The implication is that anyone can achieve the Jane Fonda physique if they have the willpower and "just do it" (in the terms of a recent ad campaign for Nike). Unfortunately, it is impossible for many individuals to achieve the aerobics' instructor look through sheer effort. No amount of effort will counter the genetic tendency for some people to have large thighs, buttocks, or hips.

Ehrenreich and English (1978) noted that women have historically been willing to alter their bodies to match the current societal conception of beauty. Because beauty is currently synonomous with thinness, it is little wonder that women wish to meet the thin ideal and, thus, appear more desirable, feminine, and beautiful. In this regard, several studies have shown that attractive women are perceived as more fem-

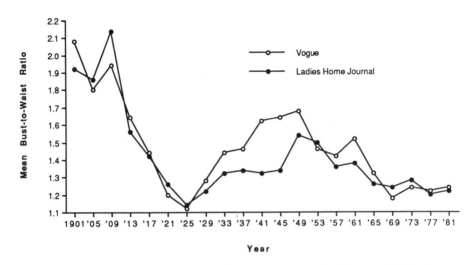

FIGURE 3.5. Mean bust-to-waist ratios of women appearing in *Vogue* and *Ladies Home Journal* at four-year intervals since 1901.

From B. Silverstein, B. Peterson, & L. Perdue (1986). Some correlates of the thin standard of bodily attractiveness for women. *International Journal of Eating Disorders, 5*, 899, Fig. 1. Copyright © 1986 by John Wiley and Sons. Reprinted by permission of John Wiley and Sons, Inc.

inine (Cash, Gillen, & Burns, 1977; Gillen, 1981; Unger, 1985). Accordingly, unattractive women have been rated as more masculine than attractive women (Heilman & Saruwatari, 1979).

It would appear, therefore, that only those women who wish to conform to the societal definition of beauty and femininity would pursue thinness. There is some evidence, however, that women who have abandoned some traditional gender roles (professional women) may have elevated concerns about body size and weight (Lakoff & Scherr, 1984). Striegel-Moore, Silberstein, and Rodin (1986) suggest that the pursuit of a thin body may reflect the general high standards that many of these professional women possess or, in contrast, they state, it may be "difficult for women to abandon feminity wholesale—and looking feminine, even while displaying 'unfeminine' ambition and power, may serve an important function" (p. 249).

Rodin et al. (1984), in an extensive discussion of cultural attitudes, cogently discuss the possible relationship among factors that may explain the sociocultural influences on body image. First, they cite evidence supportive of the stigmatization of obesity. Second, they review evidence that being attractive is extremely important in our current society. Third, they present the argument that the current female sex-role stereotype engenders a preoccupation with the pursuit of beauty. Fourth, they note that society has long reinforced the acceptance of women altering their bodies to achieve ideals of beauty (e.g., corsets). Finally, each of these facts blends to produce a society that exalts the belief that being thin is a central feature of our current ideal of attractiveness. Empirical findings support their conclusions. Rodin and Striegel-Moore (1984) found that weight and body shape concerns were the central determinants of womens' ratings of their own physical attractiveness, whereas this was not true for men.

In an interesting test of society's stereotypes of weight and shape concerns, Cash and Brown (in press) had male and female college students complete the Multidimensional Body-Self Relations Questionnaire (discussed at length in the next chapter) under three different instructional sets—for self, the typical male peer, and the typical female peer. They wanted to look at actual differences in body image across males and females, but more important, to evaluate how each sex *thought* the typical male and female would respond. There were 13 indices of body image attributes and males and females actually differed (self-ratings) on 8 of these. Females reported greater cognitive, affective, and behavioral concerns about weight. However, subjects' *perceptions* of the typical male and female differed on all 13 measures. These stereotypical views found the females to hold consistently poorer body image scores than males.

Interestingly, there was clear evidence that the distorted views were in the direction of labeling women as more dysfunctional than men. Male subjects misperceived females on 11 measures, but were inaccurate on only 4 male attributes. Female subjects misperceived females on 10 indices, but were incorrect on only 3 male attributes. In sum, women were rated as preoccupied with weight and appearance, dissatisfied with the functioning of their bodies, and uninterested in physical fitness. Most of the inaccuracies regarding men were somewhat positive—females thought the men were more oriented to and favorable toward physical fitness than they actually were. These findings partially replicate a study by Chaiken and Pliner (1987) who found that females who were perceived as eating small amounts of food were rated as more feminine, attractive, and concerned about appearance.

The results of these studies certainly indicate the power of cultural factors in shaping body image disturbance in women. However, if the above study by Cash and Brown (in press) is correct, women may not be as disturbed as, apparently, males and females think they are. Nevertheless, if the media's message remains one in which women are "depicted as worried about their weight, their muscle tone, their lifeless hair, their chipped nails, their facial wrinkles, and their visible panty line" (Cash & Brown), the time may come when actual and expected dissatisfaction are equivalent. The influence of our society and, particularly the media, therefore, is of paramount importance in attempting to explain the currently high levels of body image disturbance.

SELF-IDEAL
DISCREPANCY THEORY

As discussed at length in the previous chapter, many researchers have utilized a measure of dissatisfaction that consists of the comparison of one's ideal figure with an estimate of current or actual size. Along these lines, it is possible to conceptualize the tendency for individuals to compare their bodies in this manner as a cause of the resultant dissatisfaction with body size, shape, and/or appearance. Silberstein et al. (1987) have recently reviewed the importance of this approach. They posit that the discrepancy not only leads to a "normative discontent" with body image, but may also have an effect on other aspects of women's lives. For example, Harter (1985) has suggested that unhappiness with a particular aspect of the self will cause a reduction in overall self-esteem. The failure to match an ideal in an important domain of someone's self-definition will have much more importance than a failure in an area that is of small importance. In fact, data supports a connection between an individual's body image disturbance and lowered self-esteem (Fabian & Thompson, 1989; Franzoi & Shields, 1984; Garner & Garfinkel, 1981; Striegel-Moore, Silberstein, and Rodin, 1986; Thompson & Thompson, 1986).

The self-ideal discrepancy theory has received added support from Altabe and Thompson (1990) who looked at the relationship between discrepancy indices and other clinically relevant measures, such as eating disturbance and depression. These researchers also utilized two instructional sets to determine self-ratings of current size—an affective protocol, designed to tap into subjects' feelings about their current size and a rational instruction, geared to measure how subjects thought they looked. They found that the discrepancy between ideal and affective/cognitive ratings of body size was strongly related to other measures of body satisfaction, eating disturbance, and depression.

Much work remains to be done with this particular theoretical approach. Thus far, the work is correlational and there is no justification for concluding that women's comparison of their own size with a self-imposed ideal size is responsible for their high levels of body image disturbance or eating dysfunction. Along these lines, however, Striegel-Moore, McAvay, and Rodin (1986) found that the tendency to compare oneself to others regarding weight was one of five factors significantly related to feeling fat. It would be interesting to relate self-ideal discrepancy scores to levels of comparing the self to others. In addition, it is likely that we choose another for comparison purposes that is more along our ideal, that is, of a smaller size. The measurement of these variables would expand our understanding of the self-ideal discrepancy theory.

ADAPTIVE FAILURE THEORY

This theory deals specifically with the possibility that subjects' perception of their size may not change concurrently with their actual size change (weight loss or gain). Crisp and Kalucy (1974) thought that size misperception was an error reflecting that subjects maintained the body size perception of their maximum weight and size, thus weight loss or size change would not change their overall view of their size. The failure to adapt to change in body shape hypothesis was tested by Slade (1977) who measured self-perception in pregnant women at four and eight months of pregnancy. If the hypothesis was correct, women who were getting larger because of the pregnancy should maintain the estimations of their sizes that they made prior to the pregnancy. Slade (1977) found that women were more accurate at eight months than at four months, partially supporting this theory—if the levels of accuracy had stayed the same from four to eight months, adaptation to the changes in size would have occurred. Unfortunately, there were no measurements taken before four months, therefore the results are questionable because women may have already begun to change in size and/or shape.

In actuality, this theory has never been fully tested. To do so would require that subjects be tested at their highest weight, then followed over time to determine if reduced size is accompanied by a failure to adapt size estimations. Chapter 2 reviewed several studies that had measured the size estimation changes consonant with weight loss for obese individuals (Fisher, 1986). These findings were mixed; however, some studies did document a failure to modify estimations following weight loss. Again, it is not clear that any of these obese subjects were tested at their highest-ever weight; therefore, no real test of the adaptive failure hypothesis has been undertaken.

PERCEPTUAL ARTIFACT THEORY

A final theory has been proposed that considers the artificially minimized size of many anorexics as contributing to the data that have found overestimation to occur in this group. Because the actual size of subjects is used as the denominator in the formula to determine level of overestimation (estimated size divided by actual size), it is obvious that a smaller actual size will lead to larger levels of overestimation, even if subject groups (clinical vs. normals) do not differ on absolute estimates. Therefore, there is the possibility that anorexics' absolute estimates of size may not differ from controls.

Thompson (1987a) partially tested this idea by using controls' actual sizes as the denominator for anorexic subjects. His idea was that a height-matched control group would approximate the body shape of anorexics, prior to their weight loss. Therefore, by using the absolute actual sizes of controls in the formula to determine the anorexics' level of overestimation, he could have a direct comparison of a size-matched clinical and control group. As hypothesized, the two groups did not differ on size overestimation when this procedure was used. However, when the anorexics' actual sizes were used for the computation of their level of overestimation, they were found to overestimate to a larger degree than controls.

Penner, Thompson, and Coovert (1990) took this idea one step further and actually constructed groups of controls that were matched on actual size with anorexics. From a sample of over 100 normal subjects, the smallest actual size subjects were selected for comparison with an anorexic sample. A randomly selected group of controls was also chosen for comparison purposes. As expected, there were no differences in the level of overestimation for the anorexic and small-sized controls, but both groups overestimated more than the randomly selected controls. Thus, it appears that there is a perceptual tendency, for both controls and anorexics, to overestimate to a larger degree if their sizes are small. The Penner et al. (1990) findings are contained in Figure 3.6.

This theory has also been tested in a large sample of normals by correlating actual size to level of overestimation (Coovert et al., 1988). These researchers found that larger levels of overestimation were associated with lower absolute body sizes.

Why do individuals tend to exaggerate the size of smaller body sites? There is no answer to this question, but there are some interesting speculations. Perhaps there is an optimum range of sizes (body widths) that are accompanied by estimation accuracy, whereas, widths below (or, possibly above) the range are not perceived as accurately. This might be tested by requiring subjects to estimate the widths of many different sizes, presented via inanimate objects (for instance, bars of different lengths). Second, it is conceivable that individuals who are smaller have recently lost weight or are at a current weight lower than their maximum. If this were the case, according to the previously discussed adaptive failure theory, their tendency to overestimate might be due to

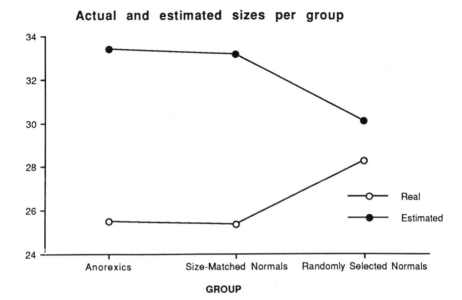

FIGURE 3.6 Estimated and actual sizes of female anorexics, size-matched controls, and average-sized controls (age range: 17–40).

From Penner, L., Thompson, J. K., & Coovert, D. M. (1990). *Body size overestimation in anorexics, size-matched controls, and average-sized controls.* Unpublished manuscript.

their failure to change their body image following weight/size change. Future research in this area would need to control for this methodological issue.

In any event, researchers in this area would be advised to closely match groups on actual body size when measuring size estimation accuracy. If this is impossible, it is advisable to equate groups statistically by covariance procedures, which allow initial differences in body sizes across groups to be removed as a confounding variable (Williamson, Davis, Goreczny, & Blouin, 1989). Otherwise, direct comparisons between groups of disparate sizes may produce misleading results.

LABORATORY MODELS
OF DISTURBANCE

In recent years, attempts have been made to manipulate variables in the laboratory and measure the effects on body image indices. These laboratory models of disturbance are of critical importance to the body image field because they demonstrate with the strictest empirical controls the factors that may operate in natural settings to cause body image disturbance. Unfortunately, the only laboratory studies have dealt with the effects of food consumption on body image. These are now reviewed.

In an early study, Crisp and Kalucy (1974) gave six anorexics and six control subjects meals that were either high or low in carbohydrate content, but matched on caloric level. Each subject received both meals, separated by a period of "a few days" (p. 354) and was assessed on size estimation accuracy before and after eating. They found that anorexics increased in level of overestimation, but only following the high carbohydrate meal. There was no difference between conditions for the controls.

In the second study to investigate food consumption and body image, level of perceived caloric content was manipulated (Garfinkel, Moldofsky, Garner, Stancer, & Coscina, 1978). Both meals were approximately 400 calories; however, one meal was "designed to connote a high caloric content; it consisted of tuna salad (136 calories) and cole slaw (87 calories) followed by a large chocolate sundae (177 calories)" (p. 489). The other meal consisted of an equal amount of tuna salad containing gluconal and mayonnaise (294 calories) and cole slaw plus oil and gluconal (117 calories). Anorexics and controls were tested following each meal, separated by a duration of seven days. They were also asked to estimate the caloric content of the meals, to document that there were perceived differences in caloric value. Both anorexics and controls believed that the "high-calorie" meal had a larger number of calories; however, size estimates were unaffected by perceived caloric level for both groups.

Freeman, Thomas, Solyom, and Miles (1983) measured size estimation changes following a meal consisting of "orange juice, cereal with milk, a bran muffin with butter, and fruit yoghurt" (p. 122) in samples of bulimics, anorexics, psychiatric patients, and controls. The meal contained 750 calories and 75 grams of carbohydrates. Eating this meal did not affect body image for any of these groups.

Chiodo and Latimer (1986) compared the responses of bulimics and controls to the ingestion of a high-calorie, carbohydrate-rich meal. Differences between the groups were evident immediately after eating and were heightened when assessed 30 minutes following food consumption. Bulimics reported feeling more irritable, nervous, and depressed than the control subjects. Although no specific measure of body image was included, it is likely that these emotional changes were paralleled by an increase in body image disturbance.

The effects of food intake on mood and body image were addressed by Robb and Thompson (1990) who tested 40 college females before and after the consumption of a perceived "high-calorie" (465 calories) or "low-calorie" (50 calories) vanilla milkshake. In actuality, the same milkshake was used for both conditions, to ensure that the foodstuff was exactly the same for both groups. The results indicated that the high-calorie subjects increased a small amount in degree of overestimation consequent to the ingestion of the food, while the low-calorie subjects became more accurate. At posttesting, there was a significant difference between groups—the low-calorie subjects were more accurate. In addition, the low-calorie subjects' level of depression improved, while there was no change in the mood of the high-calorie subjects. At posttesting, the mood of the low-calorie subjects was significantly better than that of the high-calorie subjects. Figure 3.7 represents these results.

Therefore, there is tentative evidence that food high in calories and/ or carbohydrates may have a deleterious effect on body image. This laboratory finding suggests that changes in body image consequent to food intake may be responsible for the compensatory behaviors that many eating-disordered individuals engage in following the consumption of unacceptable food—procedures such as purging or starvation. In effect, it is possible that the body image changes may be driving the negative mood changes associated with excessive food intake. However, these conclusions are premature and the entire area of laboratory

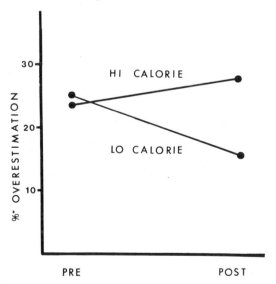

FIGURE 3.7. Body size overestimation before and after consumption of a perceived high (465) and low (50) calorie milkshake (Sample: college females, aged 17–25).

From J. Robb & J. K. Thompson (1990). *Perceived caloric content, body image, and mood.* Unpublished manuscript.

models of body image disturbance is in its infancy. These types of investigations will most likely increase exponentially in the near future. Along these lines, it would be interesting to create a laboratory analogue of teasing and self-ideal comparison strategies. Perhaps these theories might be more fully tested with experimental procedures.

SUMMARY

There are a number of theories that purport to explain the preponderance of body image disturbance present in today's world. In all likelihood, each theoretical approach reviewed in this chapter has some merit. The most supported approach, especially in terms of subjective dissatisfaction, is the sociocultural model of disturbance. It is useful to view this cause as an omnipresent, far-reaching influence on the population's concern with physical appearance. The sociocultural effect on an individual's tendency to compare the self to a societally sanctioned ideal is probably very strong, therefore a sociocultural role in self-ideal discrepancy theory cannot be overlooked. Cortical, developmental, adaptive failure, and perceptual artifact explanations are most likely not as powerful mediators of disturbance as the sociocultural variable. However, each of these approaches, especially with reference to the size overestimation component of disturbance, may account for a small, but significant portion of the overall level of disturbance. Unfortunately, the literature is notably lacking in systematic research that directly compares various theoretical approaches.

The body image literature is, however, replete with methods of assessing the multiple aspects of body image disturbance which have received discussion in the foregoing chapters. The area of assessment of body image is perhaps the most rapidly evolving subspecialty in the entire field, as researchers attempt to create psychometrically sound methods for measuring body image variables. The next chapter reviews these procedures, with a special emphasis on the practical application of assessment techniques with specific populations. At this point, the slant of the book becomes much more clinically oriented; however, important research issues in assessment and treatment continue to receive attention.

Chapter 4

Assessment of Body Image Disturbance

The construction of measurement procedures for the assessment of multiple aspects of body image disturbance has proliferated in recent years (Thompson et al., 1990). Generally, researchers and clinicians have focused on two aspects of body image: a perceptual component, commonly referred to as size perception accuracy (estimation of body size), and a subjective component, which entails aspects such as body size/ weight and physical appearance (Cash & Brown, 1987). A third component of disturbance, behavioral avoidance of specific body image disturbance-producing situations, has received very little attention, although researchers have recently constructed scales to measure the subjective report of avoidance (Rosen, Saltzberg, & Srebnik, 1990). The majority of assessment instruments that measure the subjective realm focus on the satisfaction component; however, indices have recently been constructed that also assess subjective concerns, affective reactions, cognitions, and anxiety.

This chapter offers a broad overview of perceptual and subjective measures of body image disturbance. First, the different types of instruments within each category are explained and discussed. Second, a critical review of limitations of certain procedures is presented, specifying appropriate utilization with clinical and research populations. Third, a multimodal assessment approach, emphasizing the need for a comprehensive body image assessment battery, is outlined. Finally, practical issues regarding applications with individual cases are considered.

MEASUREMENT OF THE
PERCEPTUAL COMPONENTS OF
DISTURBANCE

As mentioned briefly in Chapter 1, the onset of interest in this aspect of body image can be traced to the seminal study by Slade and Russell (1973) that located greater size overestimation in anorexics versus controls. These findings were extended and elaborated, using a wide variety of assessment procedures. In recent years, however, evidence has mounted suggesting that size overestimation is not specific to the anorexic population (Cash & Brown, 1987; Slade, 1985; Thompson & Thompson, 1986). Therefore, as evidenced from the studies reviewed in Chapter 2, these techniques are currently used in the investigation of many diverse populations.

There are two broad categories of procedures used for the assessment of size estimation accuracy: body-site and whole-image adjustment procedures. Body-site estimation procedures require that subjects match the width of the distance between two points to their own estimation of the width of a specific body site. For instance, Slade and Russell (1973) constructed the movable caliper technique (MCT), which consisted of a horizontal bar with two lights mounted onto a track. The subject could adjust the width between the two lights to match his/her estimate of the width of a given body site. The comparison of estimations with actual body widths, measured with body calipers, was used to derive a percentage of over- or underestimation.

This body-site size estimation procedure gave rise to a host of conceptually similar procedures (see Garner & Garfinkel, 1981; Slade, 1985; Thompson et al., 1990). For instance, Askevold (1975) created the Image-Marking Procedure (IMP) which requires that subjects mark their estimated body widths on a sheet of paper that is attached to a wall. Recent years have seen the creation of other innovations in assessment of size perception accuracy based on the original technique developed by Slade and Russell (1973). For instance, Ruff and Barrios (1986) designed the Body Image Detection Device (BIDD) which projects a beam of light onto a wall that the subject matches to his/her estimate of a given site. Thompson and colleagues modified the BIDD to include a simultaneous presentation of four light beams (representing the cheeks, waist, hips, and thighs) and referred to the instrument as the Adjustable Light Beam Apparatus or ALBA (Thompson & Spana, 1988; Thompson & Thompson, 1986).

For these and other site estimation procedures, an assessment of the subject's actual width (measured with body calipers) is compared with the subject's estimate, and a ratio of over- or underestimation of size is computed. Generally, the great majority of subjects overestimate all body sites; however, some data suggests that the waist is overestimated to the greatest degree (Thompson & Spana, 1988). Because the estimates of the sites are highly correlated, some researchers sum across sites, giving a generic index of overestimation. It may be advisable, given the experimental or clinical purpose of the assessment, however, to evaluate each estimation site individually. Specific descriptions, psychometric characteristics, and other information for these techniques are contained in Table 4.1.

The whole-image adjustment methods constitute a second major category of size estimation procedures. With these procedures, the individual is confronted with a real-life image, presented via videotape, photographic image, or mirror feedback. The experiment is able to modify the representation to make it objectively smaller or larger than reality. Subjects are allowed to select the figure size that matches their own conception of their image. Among the various whole-image procedures are the distorting mirror of Traub and Orbach (1964), distorting photograph technique developed by Glucksman and Hirsch (1969), but used widely by Garner and colleagues (Garner, Garfinkel, & Bonato, 1987), and the video distortion procedure of Alleback, Hallberg, and Espmark (1976). Various other permutations of these methods are contained in Table 4.1. The measure of perceptual inaccuracy is the degree of discrepancy between the actual real-life image and that selected by the subject. There are several considerations that must be taken into account when selecting and using a specific size estimation procedure—these are fully discussed later in the chapter in the section on methodological issues.

MEASUREMENT OF THE SUBJECTIVE COMPONENTS OF DISTURBANCE

The schematic figures or silhouettes of different body sizes discussed at length in Chapter 2 (refer to Figures 2.1–2.7) are the most widely used measure for the assessment of subjective components of body image disturbance (Fallon & Rozin, 1985; Keeton et al., in press; Thompson & Psaltis, 1988; Williamson, Davis, Bennett, Goreczny, & Gleaves, in press). With this methodology, subjects are asked to choose the figures that they think reflect their current and their ideal body sizes. The discrepancy between these two measures is taken as an indication of level of dissatisfaction. As Table 4.1 indicates, researchers have created many different sets of these stimuli.

Table 4.1. Measures used in the assessment of size estimation accuracy and subjective aspects of body image disturbance

Name	Author(s)	Description	Reliability[a,b,c]	Standardization Sample	Address
A). *Body Site-Estimation Procedures*					
Adjustable Light Beam Apparatus (ALBA)	1) Thompson & Spana (1988)	Adjust width of light beam projected on wall to match perceived size	1) IC: (.83) TR: Imm. (.83–.92) 1 wk. (.56–.86)	1) 159 female undergraduates	J. Kevin Thompson, Ph.D. Department of Psychology University of South Florida Tampa, FL 33620
Body Image Detection Device (BIDD)	1) Ruff & Barrios (1986) 2) Barrios, Ruff & York (1989)	Adjust distance between 2 lights to match perceived size	1) IC: (.91, .93) TR: 3 wk. (Bulimics: .82–.87 (Controls: .72–.85) 2) IC: (.21–.82) TR: 3 wk. (.34) 4 wk. (.94) 7 wk. (.37)	1) 20 normal and 20 bulimic undergraduates 2) College females	Billy A. Barrios, Ph.D. College of Liberal Arts Department of Psychology University of Mississippi Oxford, MS 38677
Movable Caliper Technique (MCT)	1) Slade & Russell (1973) 2) Slade (1985)	Adjust distance between two lights to match perceived size	1) IC: (Anorexics: .72–.93) (Controls: .37–.79) 2) IC: (Anorexics: .72) (Controls: .63)	1) 14 female anorexics and 20 female postgraduates and secretaries 2) Anorexics	Peter Slade, Ph.D. Sub-Department of Clinical Psy. Department of Psychiatry & Dept. of Movement Science Liverpool University Medical Sch. P.O. Box 147 Liverpool, L69 3BX, England
Body Size Estimation	1) Kreitler & Kreitler (1988)	Subjects, eyes closed, use the distance between their outstretched hands to indicate perceived size	1) IC: (Body: .75–.88) (Face: .79–.82) 2) TR: 2 wk. (.93–.97)	1) 240 normal males and females ranging in age from 4–30 years	Shulamith Kreitler, Ph.D. Department of Psychology Tel Aviv University Rammat Aviv Tel Aviv, 69978, Israel

58

Method	References	Procedure	Reliability	Subjects	Author/Address
Kinesthetic Size Estimation Apparatus (KSEA)	1) Cited in Gleghorn, Penner, Powers & Schulman (1987)	Blindfolded subjects adjust the distance between 2 calipers to match perceived size	1) IC: None Given 2) TR: Imm. (.45–.65)	1) 110 females aged 17–45 consisting of normal undergraduates and eating disorders outpatients	Pauline Powers, M.D. Department of Psychiatry University of South Florida Tampa, FL 33620
Image Marking Procedure (IMP)	1) Askevold (1975) 2) Barrios et al. (1989)	Subjects indicate their perceived size by marking 2 endpoints on a life-size piece of paper	2) IC: (.25–.62) TR: 3 wk. (.17) 4 wk. (.33) 7 wk. (.14)	2) College females	Finn Askevold, Ph.D. Psychosomatic Department Oslo University Hospital Oslo, Norway
B). *Whole-Image Adjustment Procedures*					
TV-Video Method	1) Gardner, Martinez & Sandoval (1987) 2) Gardner & Moncrieff (1988) 3) Gardner, Martinez, Espinoza & Gallegos (1988)	Subjects adjust the horizontal dimension of a TV image of themselves to match perceived size. Subsequent studies have also assessed ideal size and individual size estimation. Data are subject to signal detection analysis	IC: None Given TR: None Given	1) 38 Normal and obese adults 2) Normal and anorexic females	Rick M. Gardner, Ph.D. Department of Psychology University of Southern Colorado Pueblo, CO 81001
None given	1) Alleback, Hallberg & Espmark (1976)	Subjects adjust the horizontal dimension of a video image to match perceived size	1) IC: Not Applicable TR: None Given	1) 69 male and female adults consisting of obese and control subgroups	Peter Alleback, Ph.D. Furugatan SA 171 50 Solna, Sweden

Continued on next page

59

Table 4.1. Continued

Name	Author(s)	Description	Reliability[a,b,c]	Standardization Sample	Address
B). *Whole-Image Adjustment Procedures* (Continued)					
None given	1) Freeman, Thomas, Solyom & Hunter (1984)	Subjects tell the experimenter when a video image of themselves matches their perceived size	1) IC: Front profile correlation-(.62) TR: 7–22 days, frontal (Bulimics & Anorexics: .91); (Controls: .83)	1) 20 eating disordered females (bulimics and anorexics) & 20 normal females	Richard J. Freeman, Ph.D. Dept. of Psychology Simon Fraser University Burnaby, BC Canada V5A 1S6
Distorting Photograph Technique	1) Glucksman & Hirsch (1969) 2) Garner & Garfinkel (1981)	Subjects indicate size by adjusting a photograph that is distorted by 20% under to 20% over actual size	1) IC: Not Applicable 2) IC: Not Applicable TR: 1 wk. (anorexics: .75); (controls: .45). 1 yr. (anorexics: .56); (controls: .70)	2) Anorexics and controls	David Garner, Ph.D. Professor, Dept. of Psychiatry Director of Research Eating Disorders Section Michigan State University West Fee Hall Lansing, MI 48824
	3) Collins (1986)	Subjects indicate size by adjusting a video monitor fixed on their photograph	1) IC: Not Applicable TR: Imm. (.82) 1 day (.63) 8 wks. (.61)	1) Separate samples of undergraduates	J.K. Collins. Ph.D. School of Behavioral Sci. Macquarie University North Ryde, NSW Australia 2109
Distorting Video Technique	1) Touyz et al. (1985)	Subjects indicate size by adjusting photograph that is distorted by 50% under to 50% over actual size	IC: Not Applicable TR: Imm. (.82) 1 day (.63) 8 wks. (.61)	1) Anorexics and bulimics	S.W. Touyz, Ph.D. Dept. of Clinical Psychology Westmead Hospital Westmead 2145 NSW, Australia
None given	1) Huon & Brown (1986)	Concave, convex, and ordinary mirrors; adjustable TV image	1) IC: Not Applicable TR: None Given	1) Anorexics, bulimics, and controls	G.F. Huon, Ph. D. or L.B. Brown, Ph.D. School of Psychology Univ. of New South Wales Box 1, Kensington, NSW 2033 Australia

C). *Figures/Silhouettes*

Figure Rating Scale	1) Fallon & Rozin (1985) 2) Cohn et al. (1987)	Subjects select from 9 figures of various sizes	1) IC: Not Applicable TR: None Given	1) 475 male and female undergraduates	April Fallon, Ph.D. Department of Psychiatry Medical College of Penn. at Eastern Penn. Psychiatric Institute 3200 Henry Avenue Philadelphia, PA 19129
None given	1) Buree, Papageorgis & Solyom (1984)	Nineteen female silhouettes which vary in size	1) IC: Not Applicable TR: None Given	1) 19 anorexics and 19 controls	Demetrios Papageorgis, Ph.D. Department of Psychology 2136 West Mall University of British Columbia Vancouver, BC V6T 1Y7
None given	1) Counts & Adams (1985)	Silhouettes are drawn from subject's photos, sizes increased and decreased by 2.55, 5.05, and 7.55 percent	1) IC: Not Applicable TR: None Given	1) Bulimics, dieting females, formerly obese and nondieting females	H.E. Adams, Ph.D. Department of Psychology University of Georgia Athens, GA 30602
Body Image Silhouette Scale	1) Powers & Erickson (1986)	Subjects select from 7 figures of various sizes	1) IC: Not Applicable TR: None Given	1) 164 female undergraduates	Pamela D. Powers, Ph.D. Department of Psychology Academic Center Virginia Commonwealth Univ. Richmond, VA 23284
Body Image Assessment (BIA)	1) Williamson, Davis Bennett, Goreczny & Gleaves (in press)	Subjects select from 9 figures of various sizes	1) IC: Not Applicable. TR: Imm.-8 wks. (.60–.93) (Bulimics: .83 current, .74 ideal) (Obese: .88 current, N.S. ideal) (Binge-eaters: .81 current, .65 ideal)	659 females including bulimics, binge-eaters, anorexics, normals, obese subjects and atypical eating disordered subjects	Donald A. Williamson, Ph.D. Department of Psychology Louisiana State University Baton Rouge, LA 70803-5501

61

Continued on next page

Table 4.1. Continued

Name	Author(s)	Description	Reliability[a,b,c]	Standardization Sample	Address
C). Figures/Silhouettes (Continued)					
Body Build Assessment Program	1) Dickson-Parnell Jones & Braddy (1987)	A computer program allows subjects to create figures	1) IC: Not Applicable TR: Results did not differ significantly between trials	197 male and female undergraduates	Barbara Dickson-Parnell Department of Psychology Clemson University Clemson, SC 29634–1511
D). Questionnaire Measures					
1). Cognitions					
Bulimia Cognitive Distortions Scale (BCDS) Physical Appearance Subscale	1) Schulman, Kinder, Powers, Prange & Gleghorn (1986)	Subjects indicate degree of agreement with 25 statements	1) IC: (.97) (for entire scale) TR: None Given	55 female outpatient bulimics aged 17–45 and 55 normal females aged 18–40	Bill N. Kinder, Ph.D. Department of Psychology University of South Florida Tampa, FL 33620
Body Image Automatic Thoughts Questionnaire (BIATQ)	1) Cash, Lewis & Keeton (1987) 2) Brown, Johnson, Bergeron, Keeton & Cash (1990)	Subjects indicate frequency with which they experience 37 negative and 15 positive body image cognitions	1) IC: (.90) for bulimic and normal subjects for both positive and negative subscales TR: None Given	33 female bulimic inpatients and 79 female undergraduates	Thomas F. Cash, Ph.D. Department of Psychology Old Dominion University Norfolk, VA 23529-0267
2). Multi-Dimensional Scales					
Body-self Relations Questionnaire (BSRQ)	1) Winstead & Cash (1984)	Subjects indicate degree of agreement with 140 statements. There	1) IC: (.68–.91) (Males: .91) (Females: .87) for appearance evaluation subscale	Undergraduates	Same as above

62

Measure	Reference	Description	Reliability	Sample	Source
		are 9 subscales; cognitive, affective and behavioral scales for each of 3 domains-appearance, fitness & health	TR (.65–.91)		Same as above
Multi-dimensional Body-Self Relations Questionnaire (MBSRQ)	1) Cash, Winstead & Janda (1986) 2) Brown, Cash & Mikulka (1990) 3) Cash (1990)	Factor analysis of 54 items from the above scale yielded 7 subscales; plus, Body Areas Satisfaction Scale and Weight-related items	1) IC: (.75–.91) TR: None Given	2,000 adult respondents to a magazine survey	Same as above
Semantic Differential Body Image Scale	1) Leon, Lucas, Colligan, Ferdinande & Kamp (1985) 2) Leon & Mangelsdorf (1989)	Subjects rate their bodies along 16 different dimensions. Combinations of these dimensions form different constructs	1) IC: None Given TR: 3 wks. (.61–.86)	580 male & female 12th grade students	Gloria Leon, Ph.D. Department of Psychology University of Minnesota Minneapolis, MN 55455
Body Attitude Scale	1) Kurtz (1969)	Subjects rate 30 body concepts along 3 dimensions: evaluation, potency, and activity	1) Generalizability coefficients ranged from .86–.95 for the three dimensions	169 male & female undergraduates	Richard M. Kurtz, Ph.D. Department of Psychology Washington University St. Louis, MO 63130

3). Body Satisfaction/Esteem Measures

Measure	Reference	Description	Reliability	Sample	Source
Body Cathexis Scale	1) Secord & Jourard (1953)	Subjects indicate degree of positive feeling towards various body parts/aspects	1) IC: Split-half reliability (Males: .78) (Females: .83) TR: None Given	45 male and 43 female undergraduates	See Secord & Jourard (1953)

Continued on next page

Table 4.1. Continued

Name	Author(s)	Description	Reliability[a,b,c]	Standardization Sample	Address
D). *Questionaire Measures* (Continued)					
Revised Body Cathexis Scale	1) Ward, McKeown, Mayhew, Jackson & Piper (1990)	Subjects indicate degree of satisfaction with 22 of the original Body Cathexis Scale items. The remaining items were factor analyzed and divided into 5 body region subscales	1) IC: (.90 for entire scale) TR: 2 wks. (.73)	403 female undergraduates	Tom E. Ward, Ed.D. Associate Professor P.O. Box 7604 Henderson State University Arkadelphia, AR 71923
Color the Body Task	1) Huon & Brown (in press)	Subjects color an outline of a body divided into 21 regions. Red indicates liking, black–disliking, both–mixed feelings, blank–neutral feelings	1) IC: None Given TR: None Given	67 female bulimics and 67 female matched controls	G. F. Huon, Ph.D. University of Wollongong P.O. Box 1144 Wollongong, NSW 2500. Australia
Body Mapping Questionnaire	1) Huon & Brown (in press)	Subjects indicate on a 5-point scale their degree of liking for the above 21 regions	1) IC: None Given TR: None Given	Same as above	Same as above

Scale	Citation	Description	Reliability	Sample	Author Contact
Eating Disorders Inventory Body Dissatisfaction (BD) Scale	1) Garner, Olmstead & Polivy (1983)	Subjects indicate their degree of agreement with 9 statements about body parts being too fat	1) IC: (Anorexics: .90) (Controls: .91) TR: None Given	113 female anorexics and 577 female controls	David Garner, Ph.D. Professor, Dept. of Psychiatry Director of Research Eating Disorders Section Michigan State University West Fee Hall Lansing, MI 48824
Body Satisfaction Scale (BSS)	1) Slade, Dewey, Newton, Brodie & Kiemle (in press)	Subjects indicate degree of satisfaction with 16 body parts. Instrument has been factor analyzed into 3 subscales: general, head, & body dissatisfaction	1) IC: (General: .87, .89, .89) (Hand: .80, .82, .89) (Body: .79, .82, .79) TR: None Given	All females: 452 undergraduates, 463 nursing students, 40 volunteers, 169 overweight subjects, 55 bulimics & 29 anorexics	P.D. Slade, Ph.D. Sub-Dept. of Clinical Psychology Dept. of Psychiatry and Dept. of Movement Sciences Liverpool Univ. Medical School P.O. Box 147 Liverpool, L69 3BX, England
Body Esteem Scale	1) Franzoi & Shields (1984)	Modification of body cathexis scale with 16 new items. Factor analysis yielded 3 factors each for male and female samples	1) IC: (.78–.87) TR: None Given	366 female and 257 male undergraduates	Stephen L. Franzoi, Ph.D. Department of Psychology Marquette University Milwaukee, WI 53233
Body Esteem Scale	1) Mendelson & White (1985)	Subjects report their degree of agreement with various statements about their bodies	1) IC: split-half (.83) reliability TR: None Given	97 boys and girls aged 8.5–17.4 years; 48 were overweight, 49 were normal weight	Donna Romano White, Ph.D. Department of Psychology Concordia University 1455 de Maisonneuve West Montréal, Québec Canada H3G-1M8

Continued on next page

Table 4.1. Continued

Name	Author(s)	Description	Reliability[a,b,c]	Standardization Sample	Address
D). Questionnaire Measures (Continued)					
Self-Image Questionnaire for Young Adolescents-Body Image subscale	1) Petersen, Schulenberg, Abramowitz, Offer & Jarcho (1984)	Designed for 10–15 year olds. 11-item body image subscale assesses positive & negative feelings towards the body	1) IC: (Boys: .81) (Girls: .77) TR: stability coefficients for total questionnaire 1 year (.60) 2 years (.44)	335 6th grade students who were followed through the eighth grade	Anne C. Peterson, Ph.D., Dean College of Health & Human Development 101 Henderson Building Penn State University University Park, PA 16802
4). Anxiety/Concern Scales					
Mirror Focus Procedure	1) Butters & Cash (1987) 2) Keeton, Cash & Brown (in press)	Subjects look at themselves in a 3-way mirror and then rate their level of discomfort	1) IC: Not Applicable TR: None Given	Undergraduates	Thomas F. Cash, Ph.D. Department of Psychology Old Dominion University Norfolk, VA 23529-0267
Body Shape Questionnaire (BSQ)	1) Cooper, Taylor, Cooper & Fairburn (1987)	Subjects indicate the frequency with which they react in a particular way to events (e.g., worry about thighs when sitting)	1) IC: (Females: .93) TR: None Given	Bulmics Community sample Occupational therapists Undergraduates	Peter Cooper, Ph.D. University of Cambridge Department of Psychiatry Addenbrooke's Hospital Hills Road Cambridge, CB2 2QQ, England
Body Image Anxiety Scale	1) Reed, Thompson, Brannick & Sacco (1990)	Subjects rate the anxiety associated with 16 body sites (8 weight-relevant; 8 non–vant;	1) IC: (Trait: .88, .82) (State: .82–.92) TR: 2 wks. (.87)	Undergraduates	J. Kevin Thompson, Ph.D. Department of Psychology University of South Florida Tampa, FL 33620

weight relevant); trait and state versions available

E). Miscellaneous

Instrument	Citation(s)	Description	Reliability	Sample	Contact
Body Image Behavior Questionnaire	1) Rosen, Saltzberg & Srebnik (1990)	Subjects indicate the frequency with which they engage in body image-related behaviors	1) IC: (.87) TR: 2 wks. (.89)	145 female undergraduates	James C. Rosen Department of Psychology University of Vermont Burlington, VT 05405
Subjective Rating Index	1) Ruff & Barrios (1986) 2) Barrios et al. (1989)	Subjects rate body width with respect to their conception of norm for their age, height, and sex (0=much smaller; 50=normal; 100=much greater than normal)	1) IC: (.91 & .93) TR: 3 wks. (.60–.93) 2) IC: Not Given TR: 3 wks. (.94) 4 wks. (.92) 7 wks. (.58)	1) Bulimics & controls (College females) 2) Controls (College females)	Billy A. Barrios College of Liberal Arts Department of Psychology University of Mississippi Oxford, MS 38677

Key
a) IC–Internal Consistency (unless otherwise stated–Cronbach's Alpha); b) TR–Test-retest; c) Nunnally (1970) suggests that .70 is a minimum acceptable internal consistency ratio for measures currently under initial development and validation.

A recent technical improvement of the figural/schematic rating procedure involves the presentation of body schemas on a computer screen (Dickson-Parnell, Jones, & Braddy, 1987). With this method, subjects can adjust the sizes of nine body sites to arrive at the exact image representation that they believe fits their own dimensions. Again, a measure of generic satisfaction with the body can be obtained by asking subjects to create an ideal to compare with their selection of their own current image.

An entirely different procedure consists of the use of a mirror focus procedure that Cash and colleagues believe measures the affective component of dissatisfaction (Keeton et al., in press). With this method, subjects are asked to examine all their body features as they gaze into a full-length, trifold mirror, for 30 seconds at a distance of three feet. They are then asked to rate their comfort-discomfort level on a subjective units-of-distress scale from 0 (absolute calm) to 100 (extreme discomfort).

Ruff and Barrios (1986) developed a similar procedure that requires subjects to give a subjective rating of their estimated size width, presented onto a wall using the Body Image Detection Device (discussed earlier as a site-estimation procedure). Subjects are asked to judge the width of their projected beam by comparing it to other individuals of their gender, age, and height. They rate their judgment of the width of the beam on a scale from grossly below the norm (0) to grossly above the norm (100). Ruff and Barrios believe that this Subjective Rating Index (SRI) is a measure of the subjective satisfaction with current body size.

Questionnaire measures of subjective disturbance generally focus on a broader conception of the subjective component, however some scales focus fairly exclusively on weight/size dissatisfaction. For instance, Berscheid et al. (1973) developed the Body Parts Satisfaction Scale (BPSS) which lists 24 body parts that are rated on a scale ranging from extremely dissatisfied to extremely satisfied. Garner, Olmstead, and Polivy (1983) created the Eating Disorders Inventory, which has, as one of its seven scales, a subscale labeled Body Dissatisfaction. With both of these scales, subjects rate their satisfaction with several different body sites, yielding a summary score of general body dissatisfaction.

There are also many questionnaire measures that focus on the assessment of more complex representations of physical appearance. Probably the first widely used instrument was the Body Cathexis Scale (Secord & Jourard, 1953). This scale contains 46 body parts and functions that are rated on a five-point scale, ranging from "have strong feelings and wish change could somehow be made" to "consider myself fortunate" (p. 343). Kurtz (1969) used a semantic differential procedure (corresponding to Osgood's three attitudinal dimensions—evaluation, potency, and activity) in the rating of 30 different body concepts (such as color of hair, facial complexion, weight, etc.). This scale has also been modified and used recently by other researchers (see Table 4.1). Fisher (1970) developed the Body Distortion Questionnaire, which is an 82-item measure that uses a three-choice format (yes, no, undecided) to identify abnormal experiences regarding the body's function and appearance.

Cash and colleagues (Butters & Cash, 1987; Cash et al., 1986) developed the Body Self-Relations Questionnaire (BSRQ), which has three attitudinal subscales (evaluation, attention/importance, behavior) for each of three somatic domains (appearance, fitness, health). The physical appearance evaluation scale has been used extensively in research on body image (Pasman & Thompson, 1988; Thompson & Psaltis, 1988). Sample items include "I like my looks just the way they are" and "I am physically unattractive." A recent modification of this scale combined the attention/importance and behavioral subscales into an orientation domain (Brown, Cash, & Mikulka, 1990) and added subscales that deal with body satisfaction and weight attitudes (Cash, 1990a). This particular scale is widely used and has excellent psychometric characteristics—it is further discussed later in this chapter.

The Cash research group also recently developed the Body Image Automatic Thoughts Questionnaire (BIATQ), which has subjects rate the frequency of 52 appearance-related cognitions on a five-point scale (Brown, Johnson, Bergeron, Keeton, & Cash, 1990). Thirty-seven of the items are negative self-statements and 15 are positive self-statements. In a similar vein, Schulman, Kinder, Powers, Prange, and Gleghorn (1986) developed a Bulimia Cognitive Distortions Scale (BCDS), which contains a subscale that primarily measures cognitive distortions related to physical appearance. Examples of items include "My value as a person is related to my weight" and "If my hair isn't perfect I'll look terrible."

Cooper, Taylor, Cooper, and Fairburn (1987) developed the Body Shape Questionnaire, which deals with concerns about body shape. Typical items from this measure include "Have you felt so bad about your shape that you have cried?" and "Has feeling bored made you brood about your shape?" This measure taps a somewhat different construct than appearance satisfaction or evaluation. For instance, items request subjects to rate (from "never" to "always") the following sample questions: "Has eating even a small amount of food made you feel fat?" and "Have you worried about your flesh not being firm enough?"

Rosen et al. (1990) offered the first measure aimed at the assessment of the behavioral aspects of body image disturbance. Although some

items in previous questionnaire measures (particularly, the Body Shape
Questionnaire and the Body-Self Relations Questionnaire) included
questions on behavioral activities relevant to body image, neither focused exclusively on this dimension. Rosen's measure is labeled the
Body Image Behavior Questionnaire and requires subjects to rate 19
items with regard to the frequency with which they engage in certain
behaviors that prompt concern with physical appearance (such as "I
wear baggy clothes" or "I look at myself in the mirror"). There are four
subscales—clothing, social activities, eating restraint, and grooming and
weighing.

Finally, Reed, Thompson, Brannick & Sacco (1990) recently developed the Body Image Anxiety Scale (BIAS), which assesses state and
trait components of individuals' anxiety regarding weight and non-
weight-relevant body sites. Subjects' state anxiety is measured in three
different situations that are constructed to produce low, medium and
high levels of appearance anxiety. The trait measure assesses generic
body image anxiety, nonspecific to situational issues. Therefore, this
measure could be used to determine whether body image anxiety was
generalized or situationally specific for a given individual client. A copy
of this measure is contained in Appendix C.

Several measures have also been developed and validated on adolescent and child populations. For example, Offer, Ostrov, and Howard (1982) developed the Offer Self-Image Questionnaire for adolescents aged 14–18 years. It contains 130 items and 11 scales—the body
and self-image subscale can be used as a measure of general physical
appearance evaluation. This scale was recently modified and psychometrically revalidated to make it useful with younger adolescents, and
the body and self-image scale was renamed simply *body image* (Petersen, Schulenberg, Abramowitz, Offer, & Jarcho, 1984). Mendelson and
White (1982) developed the Body Esteem Scale for use with children
and adolescents (ages 7–11). This scale contains items that generally
reflect how a person values his/her appearance. It includes items such
as "I like what I look like in pictures" and "Kids my own age like my
looks." The Body Dissatisfaction subscale of the Eating Disorders Inventory has also been validated on an adolescent sample (Williams,
Schaefer, Shisslak, Gronwaldt, & Comerci, 1986) and has been used in
the measurement of body dissatisfaction in adolescents (Fabian &
Thompson, 1989). Cohn et al. (1987) have also validated the Figure-
Rating Scale (Fallon & Rozin, 1985) on an adolescent population; therefore, it is an appropriate measure for this population.

It is obvious that there are a plethora of subjective measures of body
image disturbance. An analysis of the specific content of the various
scales reveals, as discussed above, that the measures tap into many

different aspects of subjective distress. As was the case with the size estimation measures, there are many factors germane to the selection of a specific subjective assessment instrument. These procedural and methodological concerns are now discussed, followed by the delineation of a multimodal assessment plan.

METHODOLOGICAL ISSUES IN ASSESSMENT

There are several general considerations in the selection and utilization of a specific size estimation procedure or subjective measurement instrument. A discussion of the concerns with reference to the perceptual measures is followed here by an examination of issues pertinent to subjective assessment procedures. First, however, it is important to examine a basic psychometric issue that applies to all the measurement indices discussed in the first part of this chapter. As Table 4.1 illustrates, there is a broad range in the reliabilities of various instruments. Some measures do not have acceptable reliabilities and few instruments have been evaluated with different population groups. Given the criteria noted at the end of Table 4.1, it seems reasonable to exclude some measures simply because they have not been psychometrically tested or they do not meet minimum requirements for measurement reliability (for instance, a reliability coefficient of .70 is suggested by Nunnally (1970) as a minimally acceptable ratio).

With regard to size estimation assessment procedures, an essential determination for the researcher or clinician is the choice between a site-specific or whole-image adjustment procedure. Body-site estimation procedures provide information regarding accuracy that is specific to individual sites, whereas, whole-image procedures produce a single index of under- or overestimation. This is a valid choice point because research indicates that overestimation may be very site specific and not constant across all sites (Fabian & Thompson, 1989; Pasman & Thompson, 1988; Thompson & Spana, 1988). In my own clinical work, I have found that some individuals have generalized overestimation, that is, they tend to be inaccurate across all measured body sites, while other patients may overestimate only at one body site. Because clinical intervention to improve estimation accuracy (discussed in the next chapter) may be a part of overall body image disturbance treatment programs, it would seem advisable to use a methodology that would allow for the exact determination of inaccuracy. For this reason, I would recommend the use of a single-site estimation assessment procedure.

Another argument for the use of a single-site procedure has to do with the experience that patients endure when confronted with their entire image, increasing in size, as is the case with the whole-image adjustment methods. For instance, I am aware of cases that involved an individual who refused to continue with the task, given the disruptive nature of contacting a "larger" self-image. For individuals who are concerned about body image, it is easily understandable that confrontation with such an image might be distressing. Therefore, it is possible that the demands of the testing situation for the whole-image procedures may interfere with the validity of the measurement. Finally, the cost and technical expertise required of the whole-image procedures may make these procedures prohibitive for some individuals who wish to use them in a clinical setting. Table 4.1 contains a listing of addresses for the attainment of further information about the size perception indices.

There are also pertinent methodological issues that should be considered when using the perceptual procedures. For instance, the specific instructional content given to subjects may affect their ratings. It has been found that subjects' estimates are larger if they are asked to rate based on how they feel as opposed to how they rationally view their body (Huon & Brown, 1986; Thompson & Dolce, 1989; Thompson, Dolce, Spana, & Register, 1987; Thompson & Psaltis, 1988). Thompson & Connelly (1988) noted that the gender of the individual (experimenter) testing subjects might have an impact on the subjects' level of overestimation. In addition, the actual size of a subject's body appears to be negatively correlated with level of size overestimation— smaller subjects overestimate to a larger degree (Coovert et al., 1988); therefore, this subject variable may be an important methodological issue. In fact, when anorexics and normal subjects are matched on absolute size of body sites that are estimated, the groups have equivalent levels of overestimation (Penner et al., 1990). This issue of actual size being correlated with level of overestimation was discussed in Chapter 3 as the Perceptual Artifact Theory. As mentioned in that section, for research purposes, subjects of differing sizes should be compared very cautiously on levels of size overestimation. From a clinical perspective, it is important not to overreact to large overestimation levels in a small-sized individual who does not evidence other characteristics of disturbance.

Another methodological variable has been suggested by Button, Fransella, and Slade (1977) who demonstrated that the available illumination in the testing room may have an effect on size estimation procedures. They found that anorexics overestimated to a larger degree when the lights were brighter. Therefore, it is advisable for clinicians and researchers to maintain a high degree of standardization of lighting over time, otherwise this factor may contribute to changes in size estimations, obscuring the actual effects of weight gain or treatment improvements in size estimation accuracy. Researchers have also shown that accuracy may be affected by the presence or absence of facial cues and the type of clothing worn during testing (Collins, Beumont, Touyz, Krass, Thompson, & Philips, 1987a). Altabe and Thompson (in press) found that size overestimation was greater for the waist during the perimenstrual phase (menstrual and premenstrual) than the intermenstrual phase. Touyz and Beumont (1987) provide a more exhaustive review of contextual and procedural factors that may have an impact on the assessment of size estimation accuracy.

A recent innovation by Gardner and colleagues involves the use of a signal detection rating procedure as a more precise measure of size estimation (Gardner, Martinez, & Sandoval, 1987). Subjects are presented a video image that is distorted too large or too small by 6%. The subject must respond on each trial whether the image is normal or distorted. If the image is actually distorted and the subject states "yes" then a "hit" is recorded. If the body is not distorted and the subject reports that it is, then a "false alarm" is recorded. The hit and false alarm rates can be used to measure sensory sensitivity. Gardner believes that this procedure allows the researcher to separate sensory and nonsensory factors (such as attitudes and motivation level) in measurement—subjects' responses are independent of any response bias or tendency to state that the image is distorted.

With regard to methodological issues in subjective measurement procedures, it is apparent that there are many subtle distinctions between various aspects of physical appearance. Scales vary in the degree to which they primarily measure satisfaction, evaluation, concern, thoughts, behaviors, and/or appearance anxiety. Some scales are fairly discrete at tapping into one of these aspects (because of specific instructional protocols or narrowly derived items); however, other scales probably measure some combination of the above concepts. The selection of a specific scale will generally depend on the needs of the researcher or clinician. If one is interested very narrowly in overall weight/size satisfaction, the use of figures or silhouettes would appear to provide a precise measure. Subjects' selection of current and ideal sizes could be used to arrive at a discrepancy score, yielding a single index of general dissatisfaction.

It might be argued that the subjects' selection could be biased toward a larger than real figure, if, in fact, they also overestimate their size. For instance, the overestimation might lead them to choose a figure larger than they really are, thus accenting the difference between their chosen and their ideal figure. This problem might be corrected by having trained raters pick the schematic figure that most closely approximates the real size figure of the subject. For example, Keeton et al. (in press) had independent judges match photographs of subjects to silhouettes, to provide an objective measure of actual size silhouette which could be compared with the subject's own silhouette selection. However, this procedure may be necessary only if the clinician wants to use the schematic figures to assess size perception accuracy. If the figures are to be used to get at subjective dissatisfaction, the clinician would want the subject to pick the figure that most closely approximates his/her conception of actual size. The discrepancy between self-selected and ideal figure then becomes a precise index of body satisfaction. Ideally, the most information would be gained by the use of both procedures, along the lines of the Keeton et al. (in press) investigation.

With regard to figure ratings, it should also be noted that, as was the case with the perceptual measures, the specific instructional protocol may affect subjects' selection of current figure. For instance, Thompson and Psaltis (1988) found that figures chosen based on an emotional rating (subjects rated based on how they "felt" most of the time) are larger than those selected based on how subjects "think" they look. This difference between affective and cognitive figure selection may be theoretically and clinically important. For instance, this distinction may have treatment implications (discussed in the next chapter).

It would also seem advisable, when possible, to have subjects rate their own bodies on some measure of dissatisfaction (such as the Mirror Focus Procedure) rather than on some indirect index of their size (such as the self-rating of size widths represented by light beams—the Subjective Rating Index, Barrios, Ruff, & York, 1989; Ruff & Barrios, 1986). The reason for this is that self-adjusted light beams generally contain a degree of overestimation, on average about 24% (Thompson & Spana, 1988). Therefore, subjects are not producing a subjective rating of their own body or its size, but of a stimulus which, in fact, may be one-quarter larger than their own body. Hence, the subjective rating is confounded by size perception inaccuracy when this procedure is used.

One way to get around this problem, which allows for the use of size estimation procedures to obtain a subjective rating of dissatisfaction, is to allow subjects to estimate widths using instructions that ask them to rate current and ideal widths (in a procedure identical to that used with the schematic figures). For instance, Thompson and Dolce (1989) found that ideal size estimates using the adjustable light beam apparatus were significantly smaller than estimates of how subjects felt or thought they looked (in a replication of earlier work with figural stimuli, the affective instructions also produced a larger size rating than the rational/cognitive instructions). When this procedure is used, one may get a subjective measure of dissatisfaction while, at the same time, obtaining a perceptual measure of size overestimation (subjects' estimated sizes can be compared with actual sizes measured with body calipers). Thus, in this scenario, the use of the Adjustable Light Beam Apparatus (Thompson & Spana, 1988) could provide an index of size estimation accuracy and subjective dissatisfaction.

The utilization of a specific questionnaire measure will be determined by the needs of the researcher or clinician. Because of the differences in the specific aspects of physical appearance that are assessed across instruments, the assessor should be cautious against overgeneralizing the meaningfulness of high scores on a unitary index. For instance, subjects may score high on general dissatisfaction, but moderate on an index of automatic negative thoughts about appearance. Therefore, it may be prudent to use a wide variety of measures, especially in clinical situations.

The preceding discussion should serve to provide an extensive background into the most widely used assessment measures and salient methodological considerations for the selection and utilization of an assessment battery. Presented in the next section are specific recommendations for a multimodal assessment of body image disturbance.

A MULTIMODAL ASSESSMENT MODEL: PRACTICAL ISSUES AND CASE ILLUSTRATIONS

A broad-based assessment of body image disturbance should attempt to capture as many of the different aspects of dysfunction as possible. At the very least, one perceptual and subjective index should be administered. In actuality, several measures of size overestimation accuracy are acceptable; however, few questionnaires tap into several different aspects of subjective body image, including affective, cognitive, and behavioral. Specific recommendations are now offered.

As discussed above, there are several advantages of the site-estimation methods over the whole-image adjustment procedures. Among the available site-estimation devices, several have acceptable psychometric qualities and roughly equivalent costs. These include the Movable Caliper Technique, Image-Marking Procedure, Body Image Detection Device, and Adjustable Light Beam Apparatus (see Table 4.1). Cash and Brown (1987) offer one possible advantage in favor of the Adjustable Light Beam Apparatus (Thompson & Spana, 1988), noting that the "procedure, which permits the simultaneous representation of body-part estimates, would seem more valid than techniques involving piecemeal estimates, without the formation of a gestalt" (p. 506). This procedure also has large-scale norms (Thompson & Spana, 1988), which allow for a comparison of individual data with average population values of overestimation. (For further information regarding the construction and cost of this procedure, write me at the address listed in Table 4.1). In my own clinical work, I require subjects to estimate sizes using both affective and cognitive instructional protocols. Specifically, subjects are asked to rate based on how they "think they look" and how they "feel right now." Of course, it is important to ensure that subjects clearly recognize the difference between an affective state and a cognition.

A second measure that I include is designed to specifically capture the affective nature of body satisfaction. This procedure is the Mirror Focus Procedure developed by Cash and colleagues (Keeton et al., in press). In this method, patients stand in front of a mirror and rate their subjective level of discomfort on a scale of 0 (absolute calm) to 100 (extreme discomfort). Third, the Figure Rating Scale is included in my protocol. With this procedure, I require subjects to rate their ideal and currently perceived size (using affective and cognitive rating instructions).

I also use several questionnaire measures to tap into the multitude of subjective aspects of disturbance. In this regard, the Multidimensional Body Self-Relations Questionnaire (MBSRQ; Cash, 1990) would appear to be the most comprehensive and widely validated measure (Brown, Cash, & Mikulka, 1990). It contains scales that tap into affective, cognitive, and behavioral aspects of appearance evaluation, fitness, and health. It also has a specific subscale for satisfaction. The Multidimensional Body-Self Relations Scale is contained in Appendix D.

A second questionnaire is included in my protocol because of its specific assessment of behavioral avoidance situations that provoke body image disturbance. Finally, our recently developed Body Image Anxiety Scale (Reed et al., 1990) is included because it allows for the assessment of trait and state anxiety regarding physical appearance. Currently, there are no available behavioral coding systems; however, these should be developed in the near future and it would seem useful to include them in the assessment battery.

The above guidelines regarding the selection of a body image assessment battery are simply recommendations. There are obviously other measures that certain clinicians or researchers may want to use, given specific clinical questions or patient populations. For instance, with regard to adolescent populations, the use of a measure that has been validated on children is preferable. The same consideration applies to assessments conducted on males; however, as Table 4.1 illustrates, there may not be much choice in this particular arena, given the lack of standardization of assessment procedures with this population.

Another practical issue concerns the limitations present in many clinical settings, which may proscribe the use of any perceptual assessment procedure. If this is the case, I recommend that the figural ratings be used as a substitute. Whether or not assessments should be repeated and at what juncture of treatment is another pragmatic question. Several treatment studies indicate that change in body image disturbance can be quite rapid (discussed in the next chapter). Therefore, I recommend that assessments be repeated at regular intervals—at least every three months.

Additional assessment information might be gained by requiring subjects to self-monitor body image states for a period of time, during the initial stages of assessment or treatment. For instance, the figural ratings or mirror focus procedure could be completed by the patient on a homework basis, at regular intervals. By comparing these scores to situational and cognitive factors occurring concurrently with body image ratings, the clinician might glean a better understanding of specific factors relevant to an individual's case. In turn, this information might be used in the formation of an individually tailored treatment program.

Also, from an idiosyncratic treatment philosophy, it is important to understand the exact nature of an individual client's body image disturbance. For instance, in one of my cases, the woman found that her disturbance worsened after eating high-calorie foods, wearing specific clothes, or when she was around certain friends. This self-recorded information, along with an interview and assessment battery, yielded the information necessary for the development of an individualized treatment plan. In essence, although there are commonalties among individuals with body image disturbance, there is also a good deal of heterogeneity that must be attended to if an effective treatment program is to be generated.

SUMMARY

This chapter reviewed methods of assessing body image disturbance. There are a large number of extant procedures, and methods are proliferating at an astonishing rate. Despite this phenomenal interest, many instruments have not been psychometrically validated and few indices have been created for use with adolescents or males. Many procedural issues must be attended to if data from size estimation measures are to prove reliable and valid. From a clinical perspective, a broad-based assessment protocol is suggested, including a site-estimation technique, mirror focus procedure, figural ratings, and several questionnaire indices. Finally, the clinician should be attuned to the individual variability in body image disturbance and use this information in the formation of a treatment program. Optimal intervention procedures for various aspects of dysfunction are reviewed in the next chapter.

Chapter 5

Treatment of Body Image Disturbance

The preceding chapters have provided an examination of many aspects of body image disturbance, ranging from its presence in various populations to theoretical formulations of its development as well as methods of assessment. It was determined that different aspects of disturbance are present in large numbers of individuals, including individuals with eating disorders, athletes, gymnasts, dancers, and normal adolescents and adults. Given the clinical significance of the phenomenon of body image disturbance, it might be expected that intervention-oriented research would parallel assessment-oriented investigations. Interestingly, this has not been the case.

Amazingly, fewer than 10 studies (including case reports) have attempted to treat some aspect of body image disturbance. Although some general intervention programs for the treatment of anorexia nervosa and bulimia nervosa have included a component that dealt with body image dysfunction, in many of these treatment protocols, this aspect of treatment has been virtually ignored. For example, in a recent review of cognitive-behavioral treatments of bulimia nervosa, Garner, Fairburn, and Davis (1987) cataloged 22 treatment components of the 19 available treatment studies. The treatment of body image disturbance was not listed as one of the 22 intervention procedures. Rosen (1990) found that the overwhelming majority of studies either failed to target body image dysfunction or failed to measure changes following treatment.

The lack of interventions in this area is also incongruous with the views of major eating-disorder researchers, who have noted the importance of body image disturbance as a negative prognostic indicator for the recovery from anorexia nervosa and bulimia nervosa (Cash & Brown,

1987; Garner, Garfinkel, & Bonato, 1987; Rosen, 1990). As noted in our introductory chapter, Bruch (1962) went so far as to declare that progress in treatment might be misleading because "without a corrective change in the body image . . . improvement is apt to be only a temporary remission" (p. 189). She later reiterated and strengthened this view, maintaining that "patients may gain weight for a variety of reasons but no real or lasting cure is achieved without correction of the body image misperception" (Bruch, 1973, p. 90). More recently, Thompson (1987b) suggested that the "singular treatment of body image disturbance" (p. 307) might yield information relevant to the treatment of clinically diagnosed eating disorders.

In recent years, researchers have begun to take the treatment of body image disturbance more seriously and also have attempted to apply well-established methods from cognitive and behavioral psychology to this disorder. Treatment approaches are increasingly applied to non-eating-disordered populations—an advance in the field that seems to parallel the demonstration of disturbance in a wide variety of individuals who suffer from no coexisting psychopathology. In this chapter, specific treatment procedures for perceptual and subjective aspects of disturbance are addressed, followed by the presentation of an individualized treatment approach.

TREATMENT OF THE PERCEPTUAL COMPONENTS OF DISTURBANCE: IMAGE CONFRONTATION PROCEDURES

In perhaps the first study to specifically treat any aspect of body image disturbance, Gottheil, Backup, and Cornelison (1969) used a motion picture image feedback procedure with a 17-year-old anorexic. At the time of treatment onset, the woman weighed 72 pounds and was 62 inches tall. One year previously, she had weighed 116 pounds. She had begun restrictive dieting after seeing a photograph of herself that she did not like—evidently, breast development and thigh widening were two major aspects of the photo that she disagreed with.

The authors decided to combine regular psychotherapy (psychoanalytically based) with "self-image experience" (video confrontation) although the two components were administered by different psychotherapists. In the video component, the subject was taped responding to generic questions such as "How are you feeling today?" and "When did you have your last meal?" (Gottheil et al., 1969, p. 240). Then she was shown the tape of this interview. Afterwards she was asked a variety of questions, including "Who was the person in the picture?", "What was the person doing in the picture?", "What did you like about the picture?", and "What did you dislike about it?" After she responded to these standard questions (which were asked at each session) she was engaged in a discussion of her answers and asked about her daily activities.

After 16 months of inpatient therapy (including 54 video confrontation sessions), the patient was discharged weighing 98 pounds. At a two-year follow-up, she had maintained her gains and was performing well in school. Although an analysis of the specific effects of the body image disturbance treatment procedure used in this single-case study is impossible, it is useful to evaluate some of the changes in body image that she experienced throughout treatment.

Initially, the patient stated that she felt the procedures to be "stupid and a waste of time" (Gottheil et al., 1969, p. 244). Beginning with the seventh session, however, she began to report some positive aspects to the treatment, stating that "I know it has helped me to see what I really looked like" (p. 244). During the sixth month, she began to alternate recent pictures with older ones, in order to evaluate the difference between her prior appearance and current size (augmented by weight gain). She also noted that her appearance in the movie was different from her experience of her image in the mirror, noting that "When I see myself in the mirror, I feel okay, but when I see myself here, I seem too thin" (p. 244). During the latter stages of treatment, in reflecting back on her early films, she could detect herself "beginning to realize what I looked like" (p. 245).

Because the video-feedback was combined with verbal discussion (although this component was nondirective) and many other aspects of psychological intervention (including psychotherapy, dietary modification, and medication), it is impossible to attribute the patient's improvement to the self-image feedback. In fact, the patient, when asked about the procedures shortly before discharge, was ambivalent about the benefits of the procedures. The authors conjectured that the procedure may have facilitated the breakdown of the patient's denial system, forcing her to come to a more objective view of the size of her body; however, the other treatment components may have also contributed to her self-reported improvements in body awareness. In any event, the authors should be commended for their early ingenuity in the specific treatment of body image disturbance.

The second study to use video confrontation procedures did not assess changes in body image; however, a brief discussion of the Biggs, Rosen, and Summerfield (1980) investigation is warranted. In this study, anorexics, depressed subjects, and controls were given a one-shot, four-minute video viewing of themselves. The findings were quite interesting, indicating that anorexics responded to the self-viewing with a reduction in self-esteem, while the control subjects increased in self-esteem levels. The authors concluded that the depressed subjects "perceived themselves negatively both before and after video-feedback" (p. 249). Again, although this investigation offers no information regarding body image changes subsequent to video-feedback, the findings with self-esteem measures are intriguing and deserve replication.

Recent work in this area has involved greater methodological rigor and the use of controlled group comparisons in the investigation of body size feedback as a treatment for body image disturbance. Each of the following reports continues the use of a specific procedure to provide information feedback regarding an individual's body size and/or appearance; however, the focus now shifts from a whole-body image confrontation to a body-site size informational feedback technique.

Based on an earlier study by Pierloot and Houben (1978), who found that anorexics' size estimation accuracy increased when they were allowed to observe themselves in a mirror while estimating sizes, Norris (1984) used a mirror confrontation procedure with four subject groups—anorexics, bulimics, emotionally disturbed individuals, and normal controls. Norris used a procedure whereby an experimenter adjusted the length of a horizontal slit of light projected onto a wall to match the length selected by the subject as the width for a particular body site (see previous chapter, Table 4.1). Subjects estimated the following sites: head, at the widest point, waist, hips, at the widest point, and thighs, at the widest point, below the pubis.

After estimations, the lights were turned on and "the subject, stripped semi-nude, was made to face a body-length mirror" (Norris, 1984, p. 838). The subject was asked to examine her body from head to foot, paying attention to its size, "various fleshy and bony contours" (p. 838), and outlining the four sites of the previous estimations. Next, the individual (all subjects were female) was asked to describe any emotions or physical sensations that were engendered by the procedure. Throughout the exposure, the experimenter made no comments about the subject's body and did not respond to her verbalizations.

During retesting, each subject was dressed and repeated the estimations as before. However, she was told to "keep her visual and tactile impressions gained at the mirror constantly in mind" (p. 838) during this stage. The results showed that anorexics and bulimics improved significantly in accuracy, using an overall average index of change (mean of four measures). On the average, anorexics became 18% more accurate in body size perception and bulimics improved by 7.5% in accuracy. In addition, on analyses of individual body sites, anorexics improved significantly on each site. The bulimics did not significantly improve on individual site change indices. Neither of the control groups showed improvements on any measure.

In a replication and elaboration of the Norris (1984) study, Goldsmith and Thompson (1989) compared a mirror confrontation/performance feedback intervention to a contact-control group that received a general health information discussion. Subjects were normal, non-eating-disordered college females who were within 15% of ideal weight and ranged in age from 17–35. All subjects were required to overestimate (average of three body sites—waist, hips, and thighs) within a range of 21%–75% overestimation. These figures represent the bandwidth between the mean and two standard deviations above the mean for a recent normative sample of 159 subjects (Thompson & Spana, 1988). This methodological requirement was included to ensure that subjects overestimated to a reasonable degree (in the Norris investigation, many subjects were actually accurate in size perception prior to the manipulation), to exclude outliers, and to enhance the possibility that groups would be roughly equivalent on initial levels of overestimation.

Initially, all subjects were tested for accuracy using the ALBA assessment procedure (see Chapter 4, Table 4.1). Half of the subjects were then assigned to each of the two conditions. For the experimental subjects, the mirror confrontation/performance feedback intervention consisted of three stages. In Stage 1, the subject was required to face a body-length mirror at a distance of one meter, while listening to the following instructions: "Now I want you to stand in front of this mirror and take a good look at your body from head to foot. Make a full circle and examine your body on all sides. When you have finished circling, I want you to continue to look in the mirror while outlining your body with your hands and noting the various curves and contours. Pay particular attention to your cheeks, waist, hips, and thighs. Feel free to describe any emotions or physical sensations that you may be experiencing" (Goldsmith & Thompson, 1989, p. 440).

Subjects were allowed three minutes for this particular aspect of the treatment. At the three-minute mark, the experimenter asked if there were any questions. Inquiries were answered and then Stage 2 began. In this part of the procedure, subjects were given feedback regarding their size estimation accuracy. Each individual was led to a classroom chalkboard where her body width estimates were drawn horizontally with red colored chalk for each body site. Immediately beneath the estimates, the subjects' actual body measurements were outlined with a blue colored chalk. (Each of these stimuli was simply a line drawn in bold with a regular piece of colored chalk.)

Subjects were given the following instructions: "On the chalkboard in front of you are your actual body measurements in blue chalk and the estimates you gave in red chalk for each of your body sites. I want you to look at the estimates you gave and the actual measurements. Take your time viewing the board until you feel comfortable in recognizing the differences in your estimates and your actual measurements. Please feel free to ask any questions" (Goldsmith & Thompson, 1989, p. 440). Again, subjects were asked if they had any questions at the three-minute mark.

In Stage 3, subjects were again exposed to the mirror confrontation, essentially repeating Stage 1. Following the repeated exposure to the mirror, they were reassessed for size estimation accuracy. Subjects who were within $+/-$ 10% of accuracy (mean of three sites) were assessed on the Image-Marking Procedure (Askevold, 1975, see Chapter 4, Table 4.1) to test the generalization of improved accuracy from one size estimation measure to a parallel measure. Subjects who did not meet the criterion of $+/-$ 10% accuracy were readministered Stages 1-3 and reassessed. Subjects not meeting criteria by the end of three cycles of repeating the treatment were eliminated from the study (only one subject was discarded). The reason for repeated testings was to determine the power of the intervention to train subjects to accuracy. In addition, in order to test the generalizability (are changes on the ALBA paralleled by changes on the IMP) and durability (are changes maintained over time) of increased accuracy, it is important to first demonstrate a sizable effect from the treatment.

For the contact-control group the therapist read each subject a summary of material related to the topics of general health and physical fitness, including exercise, nutrition, and sleep. The subject was also engaged in a brief discussion of the topics. The amount of time spent with each subject was matched to that of the previous experimental subject (to equate groups on experimenter contact). In addition, each control subject was reassessed an equivalent number of times, at the appropriate time interval, as the yoked experimental subject.

All subjects ($n = 14$ per group) were reassessed approximately two weeks later, and a subsample of subjects from each group ($n = 8$) was assessed at an eight-week follow-up. For the entire sample, there was a significant reduction in level of overestimation that was maintained at the two-week follow-up. No changes were observed for the contact-control condition. For the subsamples, the experimental group did not differ from the control group; this lack of significance was due to the loss of treatment gains at the second follow-up phase for the experimental group. There were essentially no differences between the ALBA and IMP procedures, demonstrating that improvements with the ALBA generalized to the IMP procedure. Figure 5.1 contains the findings from the extended follow-up subjects.

In sum, it appears that positive treatment effects were found with the mirror confrontation/performance feedback procedure; however, these improvements in accuracy deteriorated over time. Goldsmith and Thompson (1989) suggested that the small number of subjects in the subsample may have reduced statistical power, hindering the chance of finding significant group differences. In support of this conjecture is the fact that, at follow-up two, experimental subjects were still 8.5% more accurate than controls. Future research with this procedure should utilize larger samples and, possibly, consider the use of booster sessions (i.e., bringing subjects back for additional treatment sessions).

Finally, in the most recent study to utilize a confrontation methodology, obese and normal-weight subjects (23 females, 21 males) were tested for size perception accuracy using a procedure whereby they could adjust their image presented onto a TV screen (Gardner, Gallegos, Martinez, & Espinoza, in press). Subjects were allowed to adjust their image to match their own conceptualization of their size in two conditions: alone and in the presence of a mirror. In the mirror condition, they were asked to use it to help themselves obtain an accurate

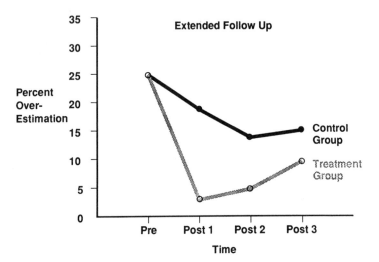

FIGURE 5.1. The effect of mirror confrontation and performance feedback on size estimation accuracy. (Sample: female college students, age unspecified).

picture of their body size. In the non-mirror condition, subjects were asked to chose their video image based on their memory of body size.

Subjects were more accurate estimators when the mirror was present than in the non-mirror condition (level of overestimation was 10.5% vs. 15.5%). Interestingly, subjects also took less time to make their judgments without the mirror (9.22 seconds) than with the mirror present (10.45 seconds). There were no significant effects for the group, therefore obese versus normal weight status played no role in the mirror's effect on size estimates.

The foregoing studies focused very narrowly on the size perception component of body image disturbance by using a discrete image confrontation procedure. In general, it appears that exposure to one's image, whether via mirror confrontation, video feedback, or specific information regarding one's ability to accurately estimate body sizes may have a positive effect on size estimation accuracy. It should be noted that research in this area is very sparse. In addition, subject samples have not always included individuals with documented dissatisfaction with their body image. This is an important issue because some investigations reveal little correlation between size overestimation and subjective aspects of disturbance (see Thompson et al., 1990, for a complete discussion of this issue). Therefore, it is essential to construct treatment programs that transcend the unitary focus on a perceptual aspect of body image disturbance. Research that is much broader in focus receives scrutiny in the next section. These treatment studies involve a comparison of multimodal interventions with subject populations selected specifically because they express a subjective unhappiness with their bodies.

MULTIMODAL TREATMENT PROGRAMS

Minimal research has addressed a multicomponent methodology targeted toward the amelioration of body image dysfunction in eating-disordered populations. However, several prominent researchers in the field have offered stimulating suggestions that are amenable to controlled investigations. These intervention procedures are here reviewed, followed by a discussion of controlled investigations with non-eating-disordered, yet body image-disturbed subject samples.

With specific reference to anorexia nervosa, Garner and Garfinkel (1981), in their widely cited review of body image, indicate that "we have found direct modification of the patient's unrealistic self-perceptions to be unproductive" (p. 279). They propose that a more advan-

procedure is to attempt to get the patient to reinterpret her ice. They attempt to get the patient to attribute her misperceptions of body size to her illness. This results in the patient's coming to question her "subjective experience in this area and ultimately function despite it" (p. 279). Garner and Garfinkel explain that this procedure is analogous to providing disability training to an individual with a handicap.

A tool that is used in the attempts to foster this reattribution of disturbance is similar to cognitive restructuring techniques (discussed in detail shortly). Garner and Garfinkel (1981) indicate that patients are encouraged to create counterarguments that foster an overriding of beliefs in the fatness of certain body sites. For example, they note that some examples of reattributions are "When I try to estimate my own dimensions, I am like a color-blind person trying to coordinate her own wardrobe. I will have to rely on objective data or someone I can trust to determine my actual size" (p. 279). In support of these procedures, they note that these subtle challenges to beliefs "help patients to understand their experiences . . . rather than deny or diminish them" (p. 279). These cognitive procedures are further outlined in Garner and Bemis (1985). Recent studies with non-eating-disordered individuals have documented the efficacy of these procedures. These studies are discussed shortly; however, it is important to first address the findings of one other group of investigators who have targeted an eating-disordered population.

Wooley and Kearney-Cooke (1987) focus on three broad components that appear to have a significant influence on body image: "incorporation of the changes of puberty, the influence of early sexual experiences, and the relationship of the mother's and daughter's body image" (p. 491). Following a focus on these issues, the patient is required to re-create their increased awareness of the developmental factors responsible for their disturbed body image. At this point, via guided imagery, patients are "asked to imagine themselves with a positive body image and to become aware of the changes that might occur" (p. 496). The final step involves requiring the patients to behave as if they had a positive body image—they are asked to "move, dress, eat, and touch themselves as they would if they had a positive body image" (p. 496). Wooley and Kearney-Cooke present data indicative of the success of these treatment techniques. However, these procedures are combined with a variety of other procedures, including, group, family, and individual therapies. Additionally, no control group is available for comparison purposes.

In the last few years, several treatment studies have evaluated traditional psychological approaches for the treatment of appearance dissatisfaction. Each of these studies has been well-controlled, including the use of control groups and of interjudge ratings to document the purity of the specific interventions. Each study was also conducted on college women, self-reporting a high level of body appearance concern, but without an accompanying eating disorder.

Dworkin and Kerr (1987) required that their subjects report a dissatisfaction with body image that also affected other areas of their life. Using the Body Cathexis Scale (Secord & Jourard, 1953), they classified subjects into groups with "severe" and "moderate" dissatisfaction. Subjects from both levels of disturbance were assigned to one of four groups: cognitive therapy, cognitive behavior therapy, reflective therapy, and a waiting list control sample. All participants attended three individual counseling sessions (counselors were six graduate students) that were 30 minutes in length.

The cognitive therapy targeted negative self-statements, attempting to modify these into positive statements. In session one, the counselor first demonstrated how to change negative beliefs about appearance into positive ones. Second, the client was taught to perform this exercise on her own. Third, homework was assigned that required the client to complete a daily log sheet, recording automatic negative thoughts, counteracting positive beliefs, and general feelings. In session two, homework was reviewed and the subject was instructed to continue with the homework assignment for the coming week. Homework was again reviewed in session three and the subject's treatment was concluded with emphasis on how the technique could be used by the individual in the future.

The cognitive behavior therapy was similar to the cognitive therapy, but also included the behavioral technique of self-reinforcement and a fantasy exercise. The self-reinforcement consisted of requiring the subject to say something positive when she had substituted a positive for a negative thought. For example, "That thought felt better, much better than the original thought" (Dworkin & Kerr, 1987, p. 137). The homework sheet also contained a column where the subject was to note the self-reinforcement used after changing a negative to a positive thought. The fantasy exercise had the subject envision "herself as a confident, competent person with an acceptable body" (p. 138). The second session included a review of the homework and the aforementioned fantasy exercise. The third session was similar to the second—homework was reviewed and the fantasy exercise repeated.

The reflective therapy involved a focus on the woman's feelings about her body during major developmental periods of her life. During the first session, an exploration of current feelings about the body, how these feelings affected the overall self, and the relevance of childhood to these feelings was undertaken. The techniques of minimal verbal following, paraphrasing, and reflection of feelings were used and the client was also asked to keep a journal of feelings. The second and third sessions were similar to the first; however, in the third session the counselor also explored what the subject felt she had learned during the treatment and how her feelings about her body and self had changed.

There were two dependent variables used to measure the effectiveness of the various interventions—the Body Cathexis Scale (Secord & Jourard, 1953) and the Self Cathexis Scale. The Body Cathexis Scale has been discussed previously (see Chapter 4, Table 4.1). The Self Cathexis Scale consists of 55 items representing self-traits that are rated on a five-point Likert scale, ranging from "wish for change" to "considering self fortunate" (Dworkin & Kerr, 1987, p. 137). The results indicated that all therapies were effective in improving body and self images. The cognitive therapy was more effective than cognitive-behavioral and reflective therapy for body image. However, the cognitive and cognitive-behavioral therapies were equally effective and more powerful than the reflective therapy for self-concept.

The finding that cognitive therapy was more effective than the combination therapy of cognitive plus behavioral techniques was surprising. The authors offered two possible explanations for this occurrence. First, the fantasy segment in the cognitive-behavioral intervention included an exercise in which subjects imagined themselves growing larger—many subjects expressed discomfort regarding this procedure; therefore, it may have actually been counterproductive rather than beneficial. Second, the cognitive procedure used counselor reinforcement for performing requested procedures whereas the cognitive-behavioral procedure of self-reinforcement asked subjects to provide their own praise. The authors concluded that external reinforcement may have been more powerful than internal reinforcement.

This study is limited by several factors. First, there was no follow-up to determine the durability of treatment changes. In addition, the second session was videotaped and rated to determine the integrity of the three interventions (i.e., to establish that therapists actually conducted sessions as planned); however, therapists were aware that they were being observed during this phase. As the authors noted, "this might have affected the manipulation check because counselors could be expected to adhere more closely to the experimental protocol during that session" (Dworkin & Kerr, 1987, p. 140). Third, the six therapists were not utilized in each of the three therapeutic conditions, rather, two therapists were assigned specifically to conduct all the therapy with a specific intervention. Therefore, a specific therapists' effect could account for the differential changes associated with the interventions. This is especially a consideration, given the differences across therapists assigned to conditions. For instance, the two therapists for the reflective intervention were slightly heavy and had red hair, while the leaders of the cognitive therapy were thin and had dark hair (no information was provided for the cognitive-behavioral therapists).

Butters and Cash (1987) provided a further test of cognitive-behavioral therapy for body dissatisfaction, including several methodological procedures that improved on the Dworkin and Kerr (1987) design (follow-up, assignment of therapists to each therapeutic condition, blind rating of session content, etc.). This study included women who scored below the 25th percentile, when compared to norms, on a widely used measure of appearance evaluation (the Body Self-Relations Questionnaire, Physical Appearance Evaluation scale; see Chapter 4, Table 4.1).

Cognitive-behavioral therapy consisted of six individual hourly sessions. Each session began with a 10- to 15-minute introductory period that included general conversation, homework review, and an overview of that week's topic. A 30-minute intervention followed (which varied across sessions), and finally, a review of the day's topics and assignment of homework.

In the first session, subjects got information about the causes, prevalence, and effects of body image dissatisfaction and the underlying rationale of the treatment program. They were also taught relaxation techniques and the use of autogenic phrases and imagery. A tape of this procedure was provided and they were asked to practice the procedures on a homework basis. In the second session, they constructed a hierarchy of body parts (moderately satisfied to least satisfied). Imaginal systematic desensitization was then used for anxiety regarding specific body areas and the body as a whole. Daily practice of imaginal desensitization was also assigned.

Session three involved the application of *in vivo* desensitization to body image disturbance. The client was guided to look at herself in front of a mirror and assigned to perform this procedure on a homework basis. The subjects were also introduced to the concept of automatic thoughts and asked to record their thoughts upon looking at their body in the mirror. Session four dealt specifically with cognitive techniques, including, the concepts of irrational beliefs and cognitive errors. Specific errors about appearance were identified and subjects selected those of most relevance to their own body. Rational counterarguments were generated to combat the irrational beliefs. Homework required that they write out specific counterarguments.

In session five, cognitive therapy procedures received further attention and subjects were introduced to the concept of engaging in behaviors that gave a sense of mastery or pleasure and viewing the body for its capabilities, not only for its relevance as an aesthetic object. For homework, they rated the frequency of involvement in physical activities and the associated feelings of mastery and pleasure. In session six, homework was reviewed and a tape reviewed the basic components of the program plus techniques for posttreatment maintenance of gains. Stress-inoculation and relapse prevention procedures were reviewed.

A variety of dependent measures was collected, including subjective indices of dissatisfaction (Body-Self Relations Questionnaire, Body Parts Satisfaction Scale, Mirror Distress Rating, Photo Self-Rating, Body Image Detection Device–Self-Rating Index and Personal Appearance Beliefs Test; see Chapter 4 for a discussion of these measures) and general psychological functioning (SCL-90-R, Texas Social Behavior Inventory—a measure that reflects self-perceived confidence, social dominance, and social competence). The results were very positive, indicating significant improvements in body image and general functioning for the cognitive-behavioral groups when compared to the waiting list control subjects. Importantly, these changes were maintained at a seven-week follow-up.

The waiting list control group received an abbreviated (three-week) version of the full treatment. The effects generally replicated those obtained with the full treatment; however, no follow-up was conducted to measure maintenance of gains for these subjects.

In a follow-up and elaboration of the Butters and Cash (1987) cognitive-behavioral approach to body image disturbance treatment, Rosen et al. (1989) used a cutoff score that was one standard deviation above the mean on the Body Shape Questionnaire (Cooper et al. 1987) as one of the criteria for inclusion in their treatment study. Subjects were randomly assigned to cognitive-behavioral and minimal contact control groups. Subjects met in small groups of three to four subjects, and therapists treated both experimental and control subjects. There were six two-hour treatment sessions for each condition.

For the cognitive-behavioral treatment, session one was an overview and discussion of body image and its development and effects on self-esteem and other aspects of daily functioning. The topic of size estimation accuracy was covered and subjects specified which aspects of their weight and size were upsetting. In session two, they estimated body size (using a body site estimation procedure) for sites that caused distress. They repeatedly estimated the size of these sites until they were accurate. Subjects also estimated their weight percentiles relative to a normal distribution. These were compared to actual weight norms. They also estimated the weight deviation of three friends whose body size they thought was acceptable. (The authors noted that these procedures were utilized to help subjects see that they were smaller than they believed and, in many cases, that they were of similar size to friends that they believed looked ideal.)

Sessions three and four focused on the concepts of automatic and irrational beliefs, counterarguments, rational thoughts, and positive self-statements. (This procedure was similar to that employed by Butters and Cash, 1987.) In the fourth session, they learned stress-inoculation training, in which they imagined encountering situations that might evoke negative body image thoughts. Sessions five and six focused on the modification of behavioral avoidance. They were asked to pick two situations that they generally avoided when upset about their appearance (wearing a tight outfit, eating dessert) and asked to predict what might happen if they were exposed to the situations. They also wrote down rational beliefs to substitute for negative predictions. They were assigned to perform homework activities that consisted of exposing themselves to the problematic situations while rehearsing the positive thoughts. Relapse prevention was discussed, and they discussed thoughts to use during high-risk situations.

The minimal treatment condition was similar to the full cognitive-behavioral condition with the exception that structured exercises were not contained in any treatment component. For example, the following elements were excluded: exercises for altering perception of body size, challenging irrational thoughts, self-monitoring forms, and assignments for behavioral exposure.

The dependent variables included a measure of size estimation accuracy, the Body Shape Questionnaire, the Body Dissatisfaction scale of the Eating Disorders Inventory (Garner et al., 1983) and the behavioral avoidance scale (Rosen et al., 1990). Subjects were assessed at pretreatment, posttreatment, and at a two-month follow-up. Analyses indicated that the cognitive-behavioral subjects had improved significantly more than minimal-contact subjects on all measures at posttesting; at follow-up these differences were maintained.

Rosen et al. (1989) concluded that the education and support components of the minimal-contact condition, without the more active practice components provided in the full treatment, were insufficient to produce a powerful intervention. They also noted a significant limitation of their study—in many cases, treatments targeted behaviors that were closely related to the dependent measures. For example, self-statements refuted during the cognitive interventions were similar to those contained in the Body Shape Questionnaire and Body Dissatisfaction Scale. Also, subjects were trained in accurate estimation of body size with the same device used to measure pre- and posttreatment size estimation accuracy. Future work in this area should consider the use of parallel measures, differing substantially from procedures and techniques used during the actual interventions.

The above treatment studies have documented a surprisingly powerful effect of various psychological interventions on body image disturbance. The procedures and techniques utilized have been described in detail to allow the reader to observe how these quite traditional cognitive-behavioral intervention strategies have been applied to a fairly new clinical problem. The next section summarizes the approaches found to be effective by the empirical studies and integrates these into an individualized clinical approach.

AN INDIVIDUALIZED TREATMENT APPROACH: PRACTICAL ISSUES AND CASE ILLUSTRATIONS

The above research investigations carefully targeted aspects of the syndrome of body image dysfunction that a thorough assessment of the disturbance had revealed were problematic. However, because most of the studies were group comparison designs, it was impossible to tailor treatment programs to a specific individual. From a clinical perspective, the idiographic approach is, of course, the optimal treatment strategy. The logic that guides my particular treatment regimen is to narrowly define specific aspects of an individual's body image disturbance, present this conceptualization of the case to the client, and create an intervention program logically based on the assessment data and conceptualization (Thompson & Williams, 1987). This may sound ridiculously commonplace, but I have found that many clinicians apply a standardized treatment protocol following their determination of a category or diagnosis for the client's presenting complaints. As discussed in Chapter 4, body image disturbance is an extremely heterogeneous disorder. Therefore, I advocate a very careful, pragmatic, application of the procedures that have been found to be effective in treating body image dysfunction.

With the above caveat in mind, I now present a brief review of the procedures that have been found to be most efficacious. First, prior to treatment, it is important to give the client some background information on the phenomenon of body image disturbance. A description of the various facets of the clinical problem, prevalence information, and the deleterious effects of disturbance on daily functioning, self-esteem, and relationships might constitute a sufficient overview. The following procedures might then be used in the formal treatment of disturbance.

Again, the blind application of all the following procedures, without first documenting that there are problems in these areas, is ill-advised.

Cognitive procedures have been found to be tremendously successful, as noted in the above studies. There are various ways to implement this approach; however, in general, most clinicians use some variant of the following design. First, irrational beliefs about the body or appearance are elicited (some of the assessment measures listed in the previous chapter are ideal for this purpose). Table 5.1 contains some sample irrational or counterproductive cognitions regarding the body. Clients are then taught to produce counterarguments—rational thoughts to challenge the disruptive and unproductive irrational beliefs. Positive self-statements could be used by clients to reinforce new ways of thinking about the body, and they might also be trained to tangibly reinforce themselves (via a contingency reinforcement program).

Behavioral procedures constitute the bulk of the treatment procedures. For instance, stress-inoculation training, in which clients imagine encountering situations that evoke negative thoughts and feelings about the body are useful. *In vivo* exposure to problematic situations—requiring them to actually confront the stimulus elements that cause discomfort—might follow stress-inoculation training. Relaxation training might be a useful adjunctive strategy when these exposure procedures are used. An interesting variation was noted by Butters and Cash (1987) who require the client to engage in coping self-statements while encountering her body in a mirror. These researchers also construct a hierarchy of body sites, by level of dissatisfaction.

Perceptual feedback procedures have also been used successfully to address the specific issue of size overestimation (Goldsmith & Thompson, 1989). This procedure, which was described in detail earlier in this

Table 5.1. Common irrational beliefs regarding body size, shape, and image

---

1. My value as a person is tied directly to my weight.
2. My appearance is so bad that I cannot let anyone see me.
3. If my thighs touch when I'm standing with my feet together, that means I'm too fat.
4. If my clothes don't fit perfectly, everyone will notice.
5. I have to weigh constantly, otherwise I'll gain weight.
6. When people stare at me, it's because I'm overweight.
7. My hair should be perfect, otherwise I look awful.
8. When I eat carbohydrates or fats, it shows up immediately on my thighs.
9. I'm special when I'm thin.
10. My overall fitness level is dependent on the amount of fat on my body—the lower the fat content, the healthier I am.

---

chapter, consists of the comparison of actual sizes with estimated sizes. It should be noted that some clients may have difficulty with the concept that they don't see themselves correctly; therefore, this technique should be carefully explained and their thoughts and feelings about the findings dealt with thoroughly. In addition, when any type of confrontation of size procedure is considered with eating-disordered patients, the clinician should take great care in making an affirmative decision. The level of denial and/or psychopathology may render this approach counterproductive. For instance, in one of my first treatment experiences with anorexia nervosa, I presented a 16-year-old female with the width of one of her thighs. She responded that it was "not my thigh, it can't be that small" whereupon I let her measure herself with the body calipers. After finishing, she looked at me and said "it's not my thigh."

Reattribution training, along the lines of Garner and Garfinkel (1981), may also be useful, although this approach has not been empirically documented and may be most useful with eating-disordered patients. Specifically, the patient is encouraged to attribute her perceptual disturbance to the illness that she currently has, not to her own perceptual abilities. Hopefully, by the continued questioning of her perceptual experience, she will "ultimately function despite it" (p. 279). As noted earlier, an example of a reattribution is "When I try to estimate my own dimensions, I am like a color-blind person trying to coordinate her own wardrobe" (p. 279). Garner and Bemis (1985) give a fuller presentation of reattribution training and also discuss cognitive techniques with eating-disordered patients that might also be applied to individuals with body image disturbance.

There are several other approaches that may prove useful with specific cases, but that have not received the level of empirical support of the techniques mentioned above. For instance, Wooley and Kearney-Cooke (1987) have found that the following three areas should be addressed: an incorporation of developmental changes encountered in puberty, the influence of an individual's early sexual experiences, and the role of the mother's body image. Freedman (1988) has also cataloged a multitude of procedures designed to enhance a woman's body image. Her book might also prove useful as a bibliotherapy adjunct to individual or group therapy. Silberstein et al. (1987) indicated that a sensitivity to the "shame experienced by women in relationship to their weight seems crucial for empathic and effective psychotherapy" (p. 104). They suggest that helping the client identify and verbalize the shame about their weight and body image is a necessary treatment component. They indicate that group therapy is extremely useful for this purpose because the individual discovers that she is not alone in her shame.

I have also found that a focus on the perceived vs. ideal self discrepancy is an extremely useful procedure. There are several ways to address this discrepancy (Higgins, Bond, Klein, & Strauman; 1986). First, it is possible to modify the individual's current ideal, making it more realistic and attainable. This might be done with the above cognitive restructuring procedures, by challenging the reasonableness of their selected ideal. Second, a reevaluation of their perceived self, emphasizing the positive qualities, as opposed to the negatives, could be attempted. Oftentimes, clients will selectively focus on one or two aspects of their body to the exclusion of the overall appearance. By broadening their evaluative strategy, it is often possible to get them to create a more reasonable self-perception.

Third, it might be useful to clarify the source of the discrepancy, possibly leading to a disqualification of the source. For instance, many individuals pick the most attractive or shapely individual available as their comparison person (the person may be a friend, but, just as likely, could be an unknown stranger or even a well-known celebrity). Using cognitive techniques, it is useful to have the individual challenge the rationality of always comparing to the "highest" ideal available, suggesting that there will always be someone who is "thinner" or "more attractive," but that doesn't necessarily mean that she is "unattractive." Additionally, it is helpful to try to get the client to reduce the tendency to compare altogether. In sum, these procedures may also be useful, although they have not been evaluated with comparative treatment research.

Finally, it is imperative that the clinician not overlook the importance of traditional psychotherapeutic process issues such as the client-therapist relationship. As I have outlined elsewhere, it is possible and beneficial to foster a trusting and empathic therapy environment when using directive cognitive-behavioral procedures (Thompson & Williams, 1985; 1987). The trust issue is of central concern, given the fact that many of these clients, especially those with eating disorders, have found that they are unable to trust their perceptions of their own body. In addition, many of the issues germane to their current body image disturbance may have their origins in early developmental time periods (Wooley & Kearney-Cooke, 1987). I have found that the occurrence of being teased at an early age about some aspect of appearance is often a historical issue that requires attention. These types of issues may require a less directive approach than the methods outlined above.

There are also some practical, nonpsychologically based, interventions that are useful with some cases, although these have received very little attention in the literature. For instance, although this issue must be handled very carefully, there are cases where the individual may, in fact, have a valid complaint regarding the existence of poor appearance. Usually these client's complaints *are* out of proportion to the *real* presence of unattractiveness. However, if, in the clinician's judgment, the client might benefit from information regarding constructive changes in appearance, such as a modification of hair style, dress, cosmetics, and so forth, I believe the client deserves this type of intervention. Again, it must be handled very sensitively in therapy and these procedures must be based on the establishment of a strong client-therapist bond.

The role of exercise is a second procedure that is useful in some cases. The beneficial physiological and psychological effects of physical activity are well documented (Folkins & Sime, 1981), and research has now addressed the effects of factors somewhat related to body image. For instance, Skrinar, Bullen, Cheek, McArthur, and Vaughan (1986) measured the effects of an intensive exercise program, consisting of running, softball, and volleyball, on body consciousness and body competence. Internal body consciousness and body competence increased, while public body consciousness did not change. Admittedly, this evidence is not compelling, and the connection between the measures of Skrinar et al. and the body image indices reviewed in this book is unknown. However, I have found that the institution of an exercise program almost universally produces an enhancement in self-esteem and body satisfaction. In all likelihood, this research area will receive a good deal of attention in the near future.

Finally, there are times when clinicians who work in the area of body image disturbance will encounter clients who wish to have cosmetic surgery. Some of these patients will be amenable to psychological interventions, but some will not be swayed from the surgical alternative. In some of these cases, the clinician may agree with the client (for example, in the case of a type of congenital problem, burn injury, or accident-induced change in appearance); therefore, maintaining psychotherapeutic contact with the client during the course and aftermath of surgery is a distinct possibility. Pruzinsky (1988; 1990a) has written extensively on the collaboration between psychotherapist and plastic surgeon and his experience with these issues may serve as a useful guide. Some of these cases, however, will not have evidence of objective deformities, but will report an extreme subjective disparagement of some aspect of the body. In these cases, the Body Dysmorphic Disorder diagnostic category should be considered. This disorder is discussed in the next chapter.

SUMMARY

In sum, there is a good deal of guidance that can be offered to the clinician who is at the beginning stages of treating body image dysfunction. However, the literature is still in its nascent stage, and many approaches have yet to be empirically tested. In addition, to date, the singular use of these techniques for body image disturbance in eating-disordered populations has not been attempted. The application of the techniques discussed in this chapter should be done carefully and predicated on a broad-based assessment designed to locate each individual client's specific expression of body image disturbance. With this cautionary note in mind, however, the clinician trained in cognitive-behavioral procedures should have little difficulty applying these techniques to the relatively new clinical problem of body image disturbance. The clinician who is relatively new to this area may wish to examine Cash's (1990b) audiotape series on the assessment and treatment of body image disturbance. His procedures are similar to many of those discussed earlier and have been shown to be effective in carefully controlled research studies (Butters & Cash, 1987; Rosen et al., 1989).

Chapter 6

Body Dysmorphic Disorder: Extreme Forms of Body Image Disparagement

HISTORY AND DESCRIPTION

In some cases, the body image disturbance is characterized by a focus very clearly on one particular site or aspect of the body and the individual reports an extreme preoccupation, even obsession, with the unacceptability of this component of physical appearance. The self-reported defect in appearance is out of proportion to the real, objective appearance of physiognomic problems. As described in the DSM-III-R "the essential feature of this disorder is preoccupation with some imagined defect in appearance in a normal-appearing person" (American Psychiatric Association, 1987, p. 255). Criteria for this particular disorder, which falls under the heading of Somatoform Disorders in DSM-III-R, are contained in Table 6.1.

The locus of the disparagement can be any aspect of the body, but the more common complaints involve the facial areas. Some of the problems that individuals find with the face include issues involving the nose, mouth, jaw, eyebrows, wrinkles, hair, spots, or swelling of the face. Pruzinsky and colleagues have recently noted that a large number of individuals request that their face/head area be made thinner or wider (craniofacial reconstruction) and have written widely about this type of body dysmorphic complaint (Edgerton, Langman, & Pruzinsky, in press; Pruzinsky & Persing, in press). In rare cases, the complaints may include the appearance of the hands, feet, breasts, abdomen, or some other part of the body. A listing of the types of physical

Table 6.1. Diagnostic criteria for Body Dysmorphic Disorder

Body Dysmorphic Disorder

A. Preoccupation with some imagined defect in appearance in a normal-appearing person. If a slight physical anomaly is present, the person's concern is grossly excessive.

B. The belief in the defect is not of delusional intensity, as in Delusional Disorder, Somatic Type (i.e., the person can acknowledge the possibility that he or she may be exaggerating the extent of the defect or that there may be no defect at all).

C. Occurrence not exclusively during the course of anorexia nervosa or transsexualism.

Reprinted with permission from the *Diagnostic and Statistical Manual of Mental Disorders, Third Edition, Revised*. Copyright 1987 American Psychiatric Association.

features that have been found to be the source of discomfort is contained in Table 6.2.

Body Dysmorphic Disorder was once referred to as dysmorphophobia; however, the latter term has recently fallen out of favor, primarily because the disturbance may not actually involve phobic avoidance. Rather, the individual with this problem might better be characterized as obsessed with the assumed defect, often spending a good deal of time and money on plastic surgery in order to correct the problem (Pruzinsky, 1990b). Because of the preoccupation with appearance, some individuals may develop an obsessive-compulsive disorder or depressive reaction. Historically, the disorder has been thought to be a premorbid indication of severe psychopathology, such as schizophrenia (Hay, 1970). Therefore, the careful assessment of individuals who present with symptoms of this disorder is essential in order to rule out other possible diagnoses (Pruzinsky, 1990b). Assessment and treatment issues are now addressed.

Table 6.2. Common aspects of the body that are problematic for individuals with Body Dysmorphic Disorder.

---

1. width of cheeks, face, or head	9. waist
2. size or shape of nose	10. buttocks
3. chin	11. thighs
4. wrinkles	12. hips
5. baldness	13. calves
6. breasts	14. genitals
7. mouth or smile	15. dimples
8. eyes or eyebrows	

ASSESSMENT AND TREATMENT
ISSUES

As noted above, the presenting symptomatology of an individual who has an extreme disparagement with some aspect of appearance may be very complex. Therefore, the assessment focus should be very broad, consisting of a lengthy clinical interview, designed to trace the historical roots of the preoccupation, utilization of traditional body image assessment procedures, and, possibly, psychological testing to aid in the determination of the presence of severe psychopathology. The clinical interview should attempt to uncover historical issues that might help explain the development and maintenance of the individual's imagined defect. In the next section, several case histories are re-created and, in each, there appears to be a logical onset to the initial preoccupation, followed by an abnormal focus on the proposed appearance defect, leading, eventually, to the development of a well-formed obsession or delusion.

The assessment measures and protocol suggested in Chapter 4 should also be used in cases that appear to meet the criteria for Body Dysmorphic Disorder (See also Pruzinsky, 1988; 1990a; 1990b). It is important to assess whether a more traditional form of body image disturbance coexists with the singular focus on one body aspect. In addition, the use of body satisfaction measures, such as the Body Dissatisfaction subscale of the Eating Disorder Inventory, (Garner et al., 1983) the Body Parts Satisfaction Scale (Berscheid et al., 1973), or questions 61–69 of the Multidimensional Body Self-Relations Questionnaire (Cash, 1990), which are contained in appendix D, may be used to corroborate the client's self-report of a singular focus on one aspect of appearance.

Because of the possible association between Body Dysmorphic Disorder and other psychiatric classifications such as obsessive-compulsive disorder, somatic delusional disorder or schizophrenia (see Hay, 1970 and Pruzinsky, 1990b, for a review of this issue), the clinician should be careful to assess for the presence of symptoms associated with these disorders. For instance, as noted in DSM-III-R, individuals who have a major depression, avoidant personality disorder, or social phobia may also exaggerate certain aspects of their appearance. However, the imagined defect is not the dominant complaint. In addition, in my experience, these individuals do not have a logical history that explains the development of the dysmorphic disorder.

In addition, in cases of anorexia nervosa and transsexualism, there may be evidence of an obsessional focus on weight and gender-related physical characteristics, respectively; however, the correct diagnosis would not be dysmorphic disorder, but the more encompassing categories of anorexia nervosa and transsexualism. Finally, although it may be clinically difficult to make this fine distinction, if the disorder is of an obvious delusional intensity, the diagnosis of Delusional Disorder, Somatic Type, is indicated (American Psychiatric Association, 1987).

There is a paucity of information relevant to the treatment of individuals with Body Dysmorphic Disorder. Because of the rarity of these cases, group outcome studies are nonexistent, and we are left with individual case studies. Given the severity of the disorder, it seems logical that many such individuals would seek surgery; however, it appears that only a small percentage do so, approximately 2% of clients with the diagnosis (Andreasan & Bardach, 1977; Pruzinsky, 1988). Therefore, although traditional medical approaches of medication and surgery have been frequently utilized (Hay, 1970), it would appear that psychological interventions might be indicated with the bulk of patients.

Accordingly, I believe that many of the techniques discussed in the previous chapter for use with body image disturbance could be utilized with the more extreme and singular appearance defect focus that is characteristic of the dysmorphic disorder. At the top of the list, I would place the cognitive techniques, followed by some of the behavioral exposure techniques (stress-inoculation, *in vivo* exposure). In most cases, the perceptual feedback procedures would not be indicated; however, if the assumed deformity was one of the size of a certain body site, these procedures might be considered. In addition, because many of these problems have an onset that can be tied to a particular situation, usually a comment directed at them from a significant other, a focus on factors relevant to the time of onset, such as puberty or the relationship with significant others (Wooley & Kearney-Cooke, 1987) might prove fruitful.

CASE ILLUSTRATIONS

My own experience with cases which have characteristics of the body dysmorphic disorder have generally consisted of individuals who distorted the size of a significant body site, for instance, the abdomen or cheeks. In one such case, the individual had a history of being teased about her cheeks when she was an adolescent. Evidently, an uncle had a predilection for pinching her cheeks and commenting on their fatness. Following these precipitating circumstances (it happened many times), she began to focus on the appearance and width of her cheeks, spending quite a bit of time looking in the mirror and trying to configure ways to hold in her cheeks to decrease the perceived width. At the time that she first came to me, she noted that the first thing she did in the morning, upon arising from sleep, was to check her cheeks in the mirror. If they looked puffy, she stated, she knew that she would have a bad day, spending a good deal of time obsessing about her looks.

Her treatment consisted of a combination of cognitive techniques and perceptual feedback. Not surprisingly, she overestimated the width of her cheeks and this information was used to help convince her that "others probably don't perceive your cheeks to be as wide as you do." The cognitive procedures were instrumental in getting her to see the fallacy of determining one's entire conception of physical appearance from a single index, the cheeks. In addition, I was able to convince her that her cheeks *were* most likely "puffier" in the morning because of the effects of sleep. She was encouraged to use another time of day for an evaluation period. We also dealt with the historical issue of the uncle's teasing. Interestingly, none of the other family members had engaged in the activity nor had any of her friends, during the formative years, commented on her cheeks. By focusing on the uniqueness of the situation and analyzing her uncle's motivations and personality, I was able to get her to somewhat disqualify the source of the original precipitating event.

Pruzinsky (1988) also describes a case that deals with the issue of the width of the face as a problematic factor. The patient had previously had cosmetic surgery for her nose, cheeks, eyes, and chin. Although she was pleased with the success of these procedures, she "stated that the one aspect of her face that was always the most troublesome *to her* was *her* perception of its wideness" (p. 10). In fact, she had developed an unusual hair style to hide the appearance of her face. The exam by the surgeon did detect a widening of the face, however, "this was not likely to be noticed by most observers" (p. 10). The individual was involved in psychotherapy that focused on her expectations for changes in her life as a result of the surgery and how her images of herself could be confronted, prior to and after surgery. The integration of the proposed surgical changes into her body image was also addressed. Satisfied that the individual was a good surgical risk, the surgeon proceeded to narrow the areas of her face that were perceived to be too wide. Pruzinsky (1988, 1990a) reviews a variety of issues that should be considered when cosmetic surgery is considered.

Hay (1970) describes a series of cases that nicely capture different types of dysmorphic clients and the precipitating factors. For instance, in one case in which a male had an inordinate focus on the size and shape of his mouth, the onset was traced to an off-the-cuff remark of his sister who noted that "You look very nice, but you have got a small mouth" (p. 402). Another female patient complained of lines under her eyes. The onset seemed to be related to her first recognition of the lines, following several nights of fitful sleep. Shortly thereafter, she began to worry that her "appearance would get worse and that if this continued she would soon look old and unattractive" (p. 404).

In some cases, the individual's singular focus on one aspect of the body can generalize to the overall appearance. Thus, there may exist times when an overall focus on body image disturbance, using the techniques discussed in Chapter 4, is paralleled by a more intensive treatment of some specific aspect of the body. In one of my cases illustrative of this example, an individual overestimated all body sites and expressed a generalized discomfort with appearance. In addition, she selectively focused on the width of the waist, from the side view. Her overall mood and selection of specific clothing seemed to be largely dependent on her state feelings about this particular site. Her treatment consisted of the general plan, outlined previously; however, part of each session dealt with her specific disparagement of the waist.

SUMMARY

The Body Dysmorphic Disorder is a relatively rare disorder that may or may not co-occur with a generalized body image disturbance syndrome. Assessment should be broad-based and concerned with the differential diagnosis of body dysmorphia from severe psychopathological conditions. Little research is available that has utilized traditional techniques as intervention strategies; however, a careful application of the cognitive-behavioral procedures outlined in Chapter 4 is warranted. The issue of cosmetic surgery is one that may arise; in these cases, the close collaboration between therapist and surgeon is indicated. Because of the large number of recent investigations that have appeared on the diagnosis and treatment of Body Dysmorphic Disorder, the clinician interested in body image disturbance can expect rapid advances in this field in the years to come (Pruzinsky, 1988; 1990a; 1990b; Pruzinsky & Persing, in press; Pruzinsky, Edgerton, & Barth, in press). The area remains a controversial one, especially when the presence of a possible dysmorphic disorder is accompanied by other psychopathology (see Thompson, 1988b; in press).

Chapter 7
Summary and Conclusions

This practitioner guidebook has examined many areas of research relevant to the understanding and clinical management of body image disturbance. An attempt was made to provide a comprehensive analysis of the current state of the field, as it now exists at the beginning of the 1990s. The last 10 years have produced a great deal of progress in the theoretical, assessment, and applied realms of a phenomenon virtually unheard of, outside of its connection to eating disorders, until recently. We now have a considerable knowledge of its etiology, manifestations, and responsiveness to intervention strategies. However, there is much yet to accomplish.

Theoretical formulations have offered some guidance toward understanding causal mechanisms; however, very few investigations have actually targeted an examination of a specific theory. Studies that compare theoretical positions are almost nonexistent. The most supported approach is the sociocultural model; however, many writers in the area offer suppositions that are not documented by data. Future research in this area is critical if we are to localize causal links in the chain that ends with clinically severe body image dysfunction. Theoretical notions should also begin to address mechanisms for the development of Body Dysmorphic Disorder.

The area of body image assessment is perhaps the most advanced aspect of the entire field. There are a multitude of measurement instruments for many different aspects of disturbance. Unfortunately, many of these indices lack psychometric sophistication and have seldom been standardized on samples other than college females. Additionally, very little research has evaluated the relationships among measures of disturbance (Barrios et al., 1989; Keeton et al., in press; Thompson et al., 1990). In addition, researchers continue to create a barrage of methods for the assessment of size perception accuracy, but few investigations have addressed the convergence between these measures (Keeton et al., in press; Gleghorn et al., 1987). Finally, there currently exists no specific instrument for the assessment of Body Dysmorphic Disorder.

Very few treatment studies have been completed; however, several of the extant investigations were extremely well-controlled and indicated positive results with directive cognitive-behavioral procedures (Butters & Cash, 1987; Rosen et al., 1989). Several techniques have also been suggested by notable researchers in the field, and these methods should be tested in the future (Garner & Garfinkel, 1981; Wooley & Kearney-Cooke, 1987). The singular treatment of body image disturbance in eating-disordered subjects, obese individuals, athletes, and ballet dancers has seldom been undertaken (Rosen, 1990). Future research should also carefully discriminate between individuals with generic body image disturbance and clients who may have a dysmorphic disorder (Pruzinsky, 1990a; 1990b).

The results of the great majority of research summarized in this book strongly indicate that the female population is at the greatest risk for developing body image disturbance. It is also now well-documented that body image disturbance is powerfully associated with eating disturbance and, in fact, may be causally related. Therefore, I believe that it is time that researchers begin to focus on two virtually ignored areas of research and application. First, we should begin to focus on the primary prevention of body image disturbance. Crisp (1988) suggests interventions with adolescents and teenagers that consist of information "about the risk factors and natural history of eating and body weight and shape disorders" and "the giving of advice and the teaching of relevant skills by direct behavioral techniques" (p. 15). I believe that the development and implementation of early intervention programs should receive our highest priority.

Second, we must begin to address empirically our societal view that women must be thin to be attractive. What mass media factors have the greatest influence on our beliefs? How can we teach people to disregard irrational expectations that are fostered by sociocultural factors? How might we intervene to change the association between thinness and acceptability portrayed in advertisements, articles, TV shows, and movies? Unless we develop answers to these questions, I see a further increase in body image disturbance in the female members of our society—and no end to their ongoing struggle to live up to an impossible ideal.

References

Agras, W. S., & Kirkley, B. G. (1986). Bulimia: Theories of etiology. In K. D. Brownell, & J. P. Foreyt (Eds.), *Handbook of eating disorders: Physiology, psychology, and treatment of obesity, anorexia, and bulimia* (pp. 365–378). New York: Basic Books.

Alleback, P., Hallberg, D., & Espmark, S. (1976). Body image—An apparatus for measuring disturbances in estimation of size and shape. *Journal of Psychosomatic Research*, 20, 583–589.

Allon, N. (1982). The stigma of overweight in everyday life. In B. B. Wolman (Ed.), *Psychological aspects of obesity: A handbook*. New York: Van Nostrand Reinhold Company.

Altabe, M. & Thompson, J. K. (1990). *Clinical correlates of body image discrepancy indices.* Unpublished manuscript.

Altabe, M., & Thompson, J. K. (in press). Menstrual cycle, body image, and eating disturbance. *International Journal of Eating Disorders.*

American Psychiatric Association (1980). *Diagnostic and statistical manual of mental disorders* (3rd ed.). Washington: Author.

American Psychiatric Association (1987). *Diagnostic and statistical manual of mental disorders* (3rd ed., rev.). Washington: Author.

Andreasan, N. C., & Bardach, J. (1977). Dysmorphophobia: Symptom or disease? *American Journal of Psychiatry*, 134, 673–676.

Askevold, R. (1975). Measuring body image: Preliminary report on a new method. *Psychotherapy and Psychosomatics*, 26, 71–77.

Attie, I., & Brooks-Gunn, J. (1989). Development of eating problems in adolescent girls: A longitudinal study. *Developmental Psychology*, 25, 70–79.

Barrios, B. A., Ruff, G. A., & York, C. I. (1989). Bulimia and body image: Assessment and explication of a promising construct. In W. G. Johnson (Ed.), *Advances in eating disorders* (Vol. 2) (pp. 67–89). New York: JAI Press Inc.

Beck, A. T. (1973). *The diagnosis and management of depression*. Philadelphia: University of Pennsylvania Press.

Beller, A. S. (1977). *Fat and thin: A natural history of obesity*. New York: Farrar, Straus & Giroux.

Berscheid, E., Walster, E., & Bohrnstedt, G. (1973, November). The happy American body: A survey report. *Psychology Today*, 11, 119–131.

Biggs, S. J., Rosen, B., & Summerfield, A. B. (1980). Video-feedback and personal attribution in anorexic, depressed, and normal viewers. *British Journal of Medical Psychology, 53,* 249–254.

Birtchnell, S. A., Dolan, B. M., & Lacey, J. H. (1987). Body image distortion in non-eating disordered women. *International Journal of Eating Disorders, 6,* 385–392.

Blumenthal, J. A., O'Toole, L. C., & Chang, J. L. (1984). Is running an analogue of anorexia nervosa? *Journal of the American Medical Association, 252,* 520–523.

Brodie, D. A., & Slade, P. D. (1988). The relationship between body-image and body-fat in adult women. *Psychological Medicine, 18,* 623–631.

Brooks-Gunn, J., & Petersen, A. C. (Eds.) (1983). *Girls at puberty.* New York: Plenum Press.

Brooks-Gunn, J., & Warren, M. P. (1985). Effects of delayed menarche in different contexts: Dance and nondance students. *Journal of Youth and Adolescence, 14,* 285–300.

Brooks-Gunn, J., & Warren, M. P. (1988). The psychological significance of secondary sexual characteristics in nine to eleven year old girls. *Child Development, 59,* 1061–1069.

Brooks-Gunn, J., Burrow, C., & Warren, M. P. (1988). Attitudes toward eating and body weight in different groups of female adolescent athletes. *International Journal of Eating Disorders, 7,* 749–757.

Brown, T. A., Cash, T. F., & Lewis, R. J. (1989). Body-image disturbances in adolescent female binge-purgers: A brief report of the results of a national survey in the U.S.A. *Journal of Clinical Psychology and Psychiatry, 30,* 605–613.

Brown, T. A., Cash, T. F., & Mikulka, P. J. (1990). *Attitudinal body image assessment: Factor analysis of the Body-Self Relations Questionnaire.* Unpublished manuscript.

Brown, T. A., Johnson, W. G., Bergeron, K. C., Keeton, W. P., & Cash, T. F. (1990). *Assessment of body-related cognitions in bulimia: The Body Image Automatic Thoughts Questionnaire.* Unpublished manuscript.

Brownell, K. D., Rodin, J., & Wilmore, J. H. (1988, August). Eat, drink, and be worried? *Runner's World,* 28–34.

Bruch, H. (1962). Perceptual and conceptual disturbances in anorexia nervosa. *Psychosomatic Medicine, 24,* 187–194.

Bruch, H. (1973). *Eating disorders.* New York: Basic Books.

Bruch, H. (1981). Developmental considerations of anorexia nervosa and obesity. *Canadian Journal of Psychiatry, 26,* 212–217.

Buree, B., Papageorgis, D., & Solyom, L. (1984). Body image perception and preference in anorexia nervosa. *Canadian Journal of Psychiatry, 29,* 557–563.

Butters, J. W., & Cash, T. F. (1987). Cognitive-behavioral treatment of women's body-image dissatisfaction. *Journal of Consulting and Clinical Psychology, 55,* 889–897.

Button, E. J., Fransella, F., & Slade, P. D. (1977). A reappraisal of body perception disturbance in anorexia nervosa. *Psychological Medicine, 7,* 235–242.

Cash, T. F. (1990a). *The Multidimensional Body-Self Relations Questionnaire.* Unpublished manuscript.

Cash, T. F. (1990b). *Body image enhancement: A program for overcoming a negative body image.* New York: Guilford.

Cash, T. F., & Brown, T. A. (1987). Body image in anorexia nervosa and bulimia nervosa: A review of the literature. *Behavior Modification, 11,* 487–521.

Cash, T. F., & Brown, T. A. (in press). Gender and body images: Stereotypes and realities. *Sex Roles.*

Cash, T. F., Gillen, B., & Burns, D. S. (1977). Sexism and "beautyism" in personnel consultant decision making. *Journal of Applied Psychology, 62,* 301–310.

Cash, T. F., Lewis, R. J., & Keeton, P. (1987, March). *Development and validation of the Body-Image Automatic Thoughts Questionnaire: A measure of body-related cognitions.*

Paper presented at the meeting of the Southeastern Psychological Association, Atlanta, GA.

Cash, T. F., & Pruzinsky, T. (Eds.) (1990). *Body images: Development, deviance, and change.* New York: Guilford.

Cash, T. F., Winstead, B. A., & Janda, L. H. (1986, April). Body image survey report: The great American shape-up. *Psychology Today, 24,* 30–37.

Casper, R. C., Offer, D., & Ostrov, E. (1981). The self-image of adolescents with acute anorexia nervosa. *The Journal of Pediatrics, 98,* 656–661.

Chaiken, S., & Pliner, P. (1987). Women, but not men, are what they eat: The effect of meal size and gender on perceived femininity and masculinity. *Personality and Social Psychology Bulletin, 13,* 166–176.

Chiodo, J. & Latimer, T. H. (1986). Hunger perceptions and satiety responses among normal-weight bulimics and normals to high-calorie, carbohydrate-rich food. *Psychological Medicine, 16,* 343–349.

Clausen, J. A. (1975). The social meaning of differential physical and sexual maturation. In S. E. Dragastin & G. H. Elder, Jr. (Eds.), *Adolescence in the life cycle: Psychological change and social context* (pp. 24–48). Washington, DC: Hemisphere.

Cohn, L. D., Adler, N. E. Irwin, C. E., Millstein, S. G., Kegeles, S. M., & Stone, G. (1987). Body-figure preferences in male and female adolescents. *Journal of Abnormal Psychology, 96,* 276–279.

Collins, J. K. (1986). The objective measurement of body image using a video technique: Reliability and validity studies. *British Journal of Psychology, 77,* 199–205.

Collins, J. K. (1987). Methodology for the objective measurement of body image. *International Journal of Eating Disorders, 6,* 393–399.

Collins, J. K., Beumont, P. J. V., Touyz, S. W., Krass, J. L., Thompson, P., & Philips, T. (1987a). Accuracy of body image with varying degrees of information about the face and body contours. *International Journal of Eating Disorders, 6,* 67–73.

Collins, J. K., Beumont, P. J. V., Touyz, S. W., Krass, J. L., Thompson, P., & Philips, T. (1987b). Variability in body shape perception in anorexic, bulimic, obese, and control subjects. *International Journal of Eating Disorders, 6,* 633–638.

Collins, J. K., McCabe, M. P., Jupp, J. J., & Sutton, J. E. (1983). Body percept change in obese females after weight reduction therapy. *Journal of Clinical Psychology, 39,* 507–511.

Cooper, P. J., Taylor, M. J., Cooper, Z., & Fairburn, C. G. (1987). The development and validation of the Body Shape Questionnaire. *International Journal of Eating Disorders, 6,* 485–494.

Coovert, D. L., Thompson, J. K., & Kinder, B. N. (1988). Interrelationships among multiple aspects of body image and eating disturbance. *International Journal of Eating Disorders, 7,* 495–502.

Counts, C. R., & Adams, H. E. (1985). Body image in bulimic, dieting, and normal females. *Journal of Psychopathology and Behavioral Assessment, 7,* 289–300.

Crisp, A. H. (1988). Some possible approaches to prevention of eating and body weight/ shape disorders, with particular reference to anorexia nervosa. *International Journal of Eating Disorders, 7,* 1–18.

Crisp, A. H., & Kalucy, R. S. (1974). Aspects of the perceptual disorder in anorexia nervosa. *British Journal of Medical Psychology, 47,* 349–361.

Davies, E., & Furnham, A. (1986a). The dieting and body shape concerns of adolescent females. *Journal of Child Psychology and Psychiatry, 27,* 417–428.

Davies, E., & Furnham, A. (1986b). Body satisfaction in adolescent girls. *British Journal of Medical Psychology, 59,* 279–287.

Davis, C. J., Williamson, D. A., Goreczny, A. J., & Bennett, S. M. (in press). Body image disturbances and bulimia nervosa: An empirical analysis of recent revisions of DSM-III. *Journal of Psychopathology and Behavioral Assessment*.

Dickson-Parnell, B., Jones, M., & Braddy, D. (1987). Assessment of body image perceptions using a computer program. *Behavior Research Methods, Instruments, & Computers, 1987, 19,* 353–354.

Drewnoski, A., & Yee, D. K. (1987). Men and body image: Are males satisfied with their body weight? *Psychosomatic Medicine, 49,* 626–634.

Duncan, P. D., Ritter, P. L., Dornbusch, S. M., Gross, R. T., & Carlsmith, J. M. (1985). The effects of pubertal timing on body image, school behavior, and deviance. *Journal of Youth and Adolescence, 14,* 227–235.

Dworkin, S. H., & Kerr, B. A. (1987). Comparison of interventions for women experiencing body image problems. *Journal of Counseling Psychology, 34,* 136–140.

Edgerton, M. T., Langman, M. W., & Pruzinsky, T. (in press). Patients seeking symmetrical recontouring for perceived deformities in the width of the face and skull. *Aesthetic Plastic Surgery*.

Ehrenreich, B., & English, D. (1978). *For her own good: 150 years of the experts' advice to women*. New York: Anchor Press/Doubleday.

Eisele, J., Hertsgaard, D., & Light, H. T. (1986). Factors related to eating disorders in young adolescent girls. *Adolescence, 82,* 283–290.

Enns, M. P., Drewnowski, A., & Grinker, J. A. (1987). Body composition, body size estimation and attitudes towards eating in male college athletes. *Psychosomatic Medicine, 49,* 56–64.

Fabian, L. J., & Thompson, J. K. (1989). Body image and eating disturbance in young females. *International Journal of Eating Disorders, 8,* 63–74.

Fallon, A. E., & Rozin, P. (1985). Sex differences in perceptions of desirable body shape. *Journal of Abnormal Psychology, 94,* 102–105.

Fisher, S. (1970). *Body experience in fantasy and behavior*. New York: Appleton-Century-Crofts.

Fisher, S. (1986). *Development and structure of the body image*. Hillsdale, NJ: Lawrence Erlbaum Associates.

Folkins, C. H., & Sime, W. E. (1981). Physical fitness training and mental health. *American Psychologist, 36,* 373–389.

Franzoi, S. L., & Shields, S. A. (1984). The body esteem scale: Multidimensional structure and sex differences in a college population. *Journal of Personality Assessment, 48,* 173–178.

Freedman, R. (1986). *Beauty bound*. Lexington, MA: D. C. Heath.

Freedman, R. (1988). *Bodylove: Learning to like our looks—and ourselves*. New York: Harper & Row.

Freeman, R. J., Beach, B., Davis, R., & Solyom, L. (1985). The prediction of relapse in bulimia nervosa. *Journal of Psychiatric Research, 19,* 349–353.

Freeman, R. J., Thomas, C. D., Solyom, L., & Hunter, M. A. (1984). A modified video camera for measuring body image distortion: Technical description and reliability. *Psychological Medicine, 14,* 411–416.

Freeman, R. J., Thomas, C. D., Solyom, L., & Miles, J. E. (1983). Body image disturbances in anorexia nervosa: A reexamination and a new technique. In P. L. Darby, P. E. Garfinkel, and D. M. Garner (Eds.), *Anorexia nervosa: New developments in research* (pp. 117–127). New York: Alan R. Liss.

Gardner, R. M., Gallegos, V., Martinez, R., & Espinoza, T. (in press). Mirror feedback and judgments of body size. *Journal of Psychosomatic Research*.

Gardner, R. M., Martinez, R., Espinoza, T., & Gallegos, V. (1988). Distortion of body image in the obese: A sensory phenomenon. *Psychological Medicine, 18,* 633–641.

Gardner, R. M., Martinez, R., & Sandoval, Y. (1987). Obesity and body image: An evaluation of sensory and non-sensory components. *Psychological Medicine, 17,* 927–932.

Gardner, R. M., & Moncrieff, C. (1988). Body image distortion in anorexics as a nonsensory phenomenon: A signal detection approach. *Journal of Clinical Psychology, 44,* 101–107.

Gardner, R. M., Morrell, J., Urrutia, R., & Espinoza, T. (in press). Judgments of body size following significant weight loss. *Journal of Social Behavior and Personality.*

Garfinkel, P. E., Moldofsky, H., Garner, D. M., Stancer, H. C., & Coscina, D. V. (1978). Body awareness in anorexia nervosa: Disturbances in "body image" and "satiety." *Psychosomatic Medicine, 40,* 487–498.

Gargiulo, J., Brooks-Gunn, J., Attie, I., & Warren, M. P. (1987). Girls' dating behavior as a function of social context and maturation. *Developmental Psychology, 23,* 730–737.

Garn, S. M., LaVelle, M., Rosenberg, K. R., & Hawthorne, V. M. (1986). Maturational timing as a factor in female fatness and obesity. *American Journal of Clinical Nutrition, 43,* 879–883.

Garner, D. M. (1981). Body image in anorexia nervosa. *Canadian Journal of Psychiatry, 26,* 224–227.

Garner, D. M., & Bemis, K. M. (1985). Cognitive therapy for anorexia nervosa. In D. M. Garner and P. E. Garfinkel (Eds.), *Handbook of psychotherapy for anorexia nervosa and bulimia* (pps. 107–146). New York: Guilford Press.

Garner, D. M., Fairburn, C. G., & Davis, R. (1987). Cognitive-behavioral treatment of bulimia nervosa: A critical appraisal. *Behavior Modification, 11,* 398–431.

Garner, D. M., & Garfinkel, P. E. (1981). Body image in anorexia nervosa: Measurement, theory, and clinical implications. *International Journal of Psychiatry in Medicine, 11,* 263–284.

Garner, D. M., Garfinkel, P. E., & Bonato, D. P. (1987). Body image measurement in eating disorders. *Advances in Psychosomatic Medicine, 17,* 119–133.

Garner, D. M., Garfinkel, P. E., Rockert, W., & Olmsted, M. P. (1987). A prospective study of eating disturbances in the ballet. *Psychotherapy and Psychosomatics, 48,* 170–175.

Garner, D. M., Garfinkel, P. E., Schwartz, D., & Thompson, M. (1980). Cultural expectations of thinness in women. *Psychological Reports, 47,* 483–491.

Garner, D. M., Garfinkel, P. E., Stancer, H. C., & Moldofsky, H. (1976). Body image disturbance in anorexia nervosa and obesity. *Psychosomatic Medicine, 38,* 329–336.

Garner, D. M., Olmstead, M. A., & Polivy, J. (1983). Development and validation of a multidimensional eating disorder inventory for anorexia nervosa and bulimia. *International Journal of Eating Disorders, 2,* 15–34.

Gillen, B. (1981). Physical attractiveness: A determinant of two types of goodness. *Personality and Social Psychology Bulletin, 7,* 277–281.

Gleghorn, A. A., Penner, L. A., Powers, P. S., & Schulman, R. (1987). The psychometric properties of several measures of body image. *Journal of Psychopathology and Behavioral Assessment, 9,* 203–218.

Glucksman, M., & Hirsch, J. (1969). The response of obese patients to weight reduction. III. The perception of body size. *Psychosomatic Medicine, 31,* 1–17.

Goldsmith, D., & Thompson, J. K. (1989). The effect of mirror confrontation and size estimation accuracy feedback on perceptual inaccuracy in normal females who overestimate body size. *International Journal of Eating Disorders, 8,* 437–444.

Gottheil, E., Backup, C. E., & Cornelison, F. S. (1969). Denial and self-image confrontation in a case of anorexia nervosa. *The Journal of Nervous and Mental Disease, 148,* 238–250.

Grant, C. L., & Fodor, I. G. (1986). Adolescent attitudes toward body image and anorexic behavior. *Adolescence, 21,* 269–281.

Grinker, J. (1973). Behavioral and metabolic consequences of weight reduction. *Journal of the American Dietetic Association, 62,* 30–34.

Gross, J., & Rosen, J. C. (1988). Bulimia in adolescents: Prevalence and psychosocial correlates. *International Journal of Eating Disorders, 7,* 51–61.

Halmi, K. A., Goldberg, S. C., & Cunningham, S. (1977). Perceptual distortion of body image in adolescent girls: Distortion of body image in adolescence. *Psychological Medicine, 7,* 253–257.

Hamilton, L. H., Brooks-Gunn, J., & Warren, M. P. (1985). Sociocultural influences on eating disorders in professional female ballet dancers. *International Journal of Eating Disorders, 4,* 465–477.

Hamilton, L. H., Brooks-Gunn, J., Warren, M. P., & Hamilton, W. G. (1988). The role of selectivity in the pathogenesis of eating problems in ballet dancers. *Medicine and Science in Sports and Exercise, 20,* 560–565.

Harter, S. (1985). Processes underlying the construction, maintenance, and enhancement of the self-concept in children. In J. Suls & A. Greenwald (Eds.), *Psychological perspectives on the self* (pp. 137–181). Hillsdale, NJ: Lawrence Erlbaum Associates.

Hatfield, E., & Sprecher, S. (1986). *Mirror, mirror, on the wall.* New York: SUNY Press.

Hawkins, R. C. II, & Clement, P. F. (1984). Binge eating: Measurement problems and a conceptual model. In R. C. Hawkins II, W. J. Fremouw, & P. F. Clement (Eds.), *The binge-purge syndrome* (pp. 229–253). New York: Springer.

Hay, G. G. (1970). Dysmorphophobia. *British Journal of Psychiatry, 116,* 399–406.

Heilman, M. E., & Saruwatari, L. R. (1979). When beauty is beastly: The effects of appearance and sex on evaluations of job applicants for managerial and nonmanagerial jobs. *Organizational Behavior, 23,* 360–372.

Hesse-Biber, S., Clayton-Matthews, A., & Downey, J. A. (1988). The differential importance of weight and body image among college men and women. *Genetic, Social, and General Psychology Monographs, 114,* 511–528.

Higgins, E. T., Bond, R. N., Klein, R., & Strauman, T. (1986). Self-discrepancies and emotional vulnerability: How magnitude, accessibility, and type of discrepancy influence affect. *Journal of Personality and Social Psychology, 51,* 5–15.

Hsu, L. K. G. (1982). Is there a disturbance in body image in anorexia nervosa? *The Journal of Nervous and Mental Disease, 170,* 305–307.

Hsu, L. K. G. (1989). The gender gap in eating disorders: Why are the eating disorders more common among women? *Clinical Psychology Review, 9,* 393–407.

Huon, G. F., & Brown, L. B. (1986). Body image in anorexia nervosa and bulimia nervosa. *International Journal of Eating Disorders, 5,* 421–439.

Huon, G. F., & Brown, L. B. (in press). Assessing bulimics' dissatisfaction with their body. *British Journal of Clinical Psychology.*

Keeton, W. P., Cash, T. F., & Brown, T. A. (in press). The multidimensional assessment of body image among college students. *Sex Roles.*

Knight, P. O., Schocken, D. D., Powers, P. S., Feld, J., & Smith, J. T. (1987). Gender comparison in anorexia nervosa and obligate running (Abstract). *Medicine and Science in Sports and Exercise, 19,* S66.

Koff, E., Rierdan, J., & Silverstone, E. (1978). Changes in representation of body image as a function of menarcheal status. *Developmental Psychology, 14,* 635–642.

Kowalski, P. S. (1986). Cognitive abilities of female adolescents with anorexia nervosa. *International Journal of Eating Disorders, 5,* 983–998.

Kreitler, S., & Kreitler, H. (1988). Body image: The dimension of size. *Genetic, Social, and General Psychology Monographs, 114,* 7–32.

Kurtz, R. M. (1969). Sex differences and variations in body attitudes. *Journal of Consulting and Clinical Psychology, 33,* 625–629.

Lacey, J. H., & Birtchnell, S. A. (1986). Body image and its disturbances. *Journal of Psychosomatic Research, 30,* 623–631.

Lakoff, R. T., & Scherr, R. L. (1984). *Face value: The politics of beauty.* Boston: Routledge & Kegan Paul.

Leon, G. R., Lucas, A. R., Colligan, R. C., Ferdinande, R. J., & Kamp, J. (1985). Sexual, body-image, and personality attitudes in anorexia nervosa. *Journal of Abnormal Child Psychology, 13,* 245–258.

Leon, G. R., & Mangelsdorf, C. (1989). *The semantic-differential body image scale.* Unpublished manuscript.

Lerner, R. M., Orlos, J. B., & Knapp, J. R. (1976). Physical attractiveness, physical effectiveness, and self-concept in late adolescence. *Adolescence, 11,* 313–326.

Lindholm, L., & Wilson, G. T. (1988). Body image assessment in patients with bulimia nervosa and normal controls. *International Journal of Eating Disorders, 7,* 527–539.

Marino, D. D., & King, J. C. (1980). Nutritional concerns during adolescence. *Pediatric Clinics of North America, 27,* 125–139.

Marsella, A. J., Shizuru, L., Brennan, J., & Kameoka, V. (1981). Depression and body image satisfaction. *Journal of Cross-Cultural Psychology, 12,* 360–371.

McCrea, W., Summerfield, A. B., & Rosen, B. (1982). Body image: A selective review of existing measurement techniques. *British Journal of Medical Psychology, 55,* 225–233.

Meermann, R. (1983). Experimental investigation of disturbances in body image estimation in anorexia nervosa patients, and ballet and gymnastics pupils. *International Journal of Eating Disorders, 2,* 91–100.

Mendelson, B. K., & White, D. R. (1982). Relation between body-esteem and self-esteem of obese and normal children. *Perceptual and Motor Skills, 54,* 899–905.

Mendelson, B. K., & White, D. R. (1985). Development of self-body-esteem in overweight youngsters. *Developmental Psychology, 21,* 90–96.

Nielson, A. C. (1979). *Who is dieting and why?* Chicago, IL: Nielson Company, Research Department.

Noles, S. W., Cash, T. F., & Winstead, B. A. (1985). Body image, physical attractiveness, and depression. *Journal of Consulting and Clinical Psychology, 53,* 88–94.

Norris, D. L. (1984). The effects of mirror confrontation on self-estimation of body dimensions in anorexia nervosa, bulimia, and two control groups. *Psychological Medicine, 14,* 835–842.

Nudelman, S., Rosen, J. C., & Leitenberg, H. (1988). Dissimilarities in eating attitudes, body image distortion, depression, and self-esteem between high-intensity male runners and women with bulimia nervosa. *International Journal of Eating Disorders, 7,* 625–634.

Nunnally, J. (1970). *Psychometric theory.* New York: McGraw-Hill.

Offer, D., Ostrov, E., & Howard, K., I. (1982). *The Offer Self-Image Questionnaire for Adolescents: A Manual,* 3rd ed., Michael Reese Hospital, Chicago.

Owens, R. G., & Slade, P. D. (1987). Running and anorexia nervosa: An empirical study. *International Journal of Eating Disorders, 6,* 771–775.

Pasman, L., & Thompson, J. K. (1988). Body image and eating disturbance in obligatory runners, obligatory weightlifters, and sedentary individuals. *International Journal of Eating Disorders, 7,* 759–770.

Penner, L., Thompson, J. K., & Coovert, D. L. (1990). *The effect of actual body size on size estimation accuracy in anorexics, size-matched controls, and randomly selected controls.* Unpublished manuscript.

Peskin, H. (1973). Influence of the developmental schedule of puberty on learning and ego functioning. *Journal of Youth and Adolescence, 2,* 273–290.

Peterson, A. C., Schulenberg, J. E., Abramowitz, R. H., Offer, D., & Jarcho, H. D. (1984). A self-image questionnaire for young adolescents (SIQYA): Reliability and validity studies. *Journal of Youth and Adolescence, 13,* 93–111.

Pierloot, R. A., & Houben, M. E. (1978). Estimation of body dimensions in anorexia nervosa. *Psychological Medicine, 8,* 317–324.

Post, G., & Crowther, J. H. (1987). Restricter-purger differences in bulimic adolescent females. *International Journal of Eating Disorders, 6,* 757–762.

Powers, P. D., & Erickson, M. T. (1986). Body-image in women and its relationship to self-image and body satisfaction. *The Journal of Obesity and Weight Regulation, 5,* 37–50.

Pruzinsky, T. (1988). Collaboration of plastic surgeon and medical psychotherapist: Elective cosmetic surgery. *Medical Psychotherapy, 1,* 1–13.

Pruzinsky, T. (1990a). Personality change in cosmetic plastic surgery. In T. F. Cash & T. Pruzinsky (Eds.), *Body images: Development, deviance, and change.* New York: Guilford.

Pruzinsky, T. (1990b). Body experience psychopathology. In T. F. Cash & T. Pruzinsky (Eds.), *Body images: Development, deviance, and change.* New York: Guilford.

Pruzinsky, T., Edgerton, M. T., & Barth, J. T. (in press). Medical psychotherapy and plastic surgery: Collaboration, specialization and cost-effectiveness. In K. Anchor (Ed.) *The handbook of medical psychotherapy.* Toronto: Hans Huber Publishers.

Pruzinsky, T., & Persing, J. (in press). Psychological perspectives on aesthetic applications of reconstructive surgery techniques. In D. K. Ousterhout (Ed.). *Aesthetic applications of craniofacial techniques.* Boston: Little, Brown & Co.

Reed, D., Thompson, J. K., Brannick, M., & Sacco, W. (1990). *The State and Trait Body Image Anxiety Scale.* Unpublished manuscript.

Richards, K. J., Thompson, J. K., & Coovert, M. (1990). *Development of body image and eating disturbance.* Unpublished manuscript.

Robb, J., & Thompson, J. K. (1990). *Perceived caloric content, body image, and mood.* Unpublished manuscript.

Rodin, J., Silberstein, L. R., & Striegel-Moore, R. H. (1985). Women and weight: A normative discontent. In T. B. Sonderegger (Ed.), *Psychology and Gender. Nebraska Symposium on Motivation, 1984* (pp. 267–307). Lincoln: University of Nebraska Press.

Rodin, J., & Striegel-Moore, R. H. (1984, September). *Predicting attitudes toward body weight and food intake in women.* Paper presented at the 14th Congress of the European Association of Behavior Therapy.

Rosen, J. C. (1990). Body image disturbances in eating disorders. In T. F. Cash and T. Pruzinsky (Eds.), *Body images: Development, deviance, and change.* New York: Guilford.

Rosen, J. C., Saltzberg, E., & Srebnik, D. (1989). Cognitive behavior therapy for negative body image. *Behavior Therapy, 20,* 393–404.

Rosen, J. C., Saltzberg, E., & Srebnik, D. (1990). *Development of a body image behavior questionnaire.* Unpublished manuscript.

Rothblum, E. D., Miller, C. T., & Garbutt, B. (1988). Stereotypes of obese female job applicants. *International Journal of Eating Disorders, 7,* 277–284.

Rozin, P., & Fallon, A. (1988). Body image, attitudes to weight, and misperceptions of figure preferences of the opposite sex: A comparison of men and women in two generations. *Journal of Abnormal Psychology, 97,* 342–345.

Ruff, G. A., & Barrios, B. A. (1986). Realistic assessment of body image. *Behavioral Assessment, 8,* 237–252.

Scalf-McIver, L., & Thompson, J. K. (1989). Family correlates of bulimic characteristics in college females. *Journal of Clinical Psychology, 45,* 473–478.

Schulman, R. G., Kinder, B. N., Powers, P. S., Prange, M., & Gleghorn, A. A. (1986). The development of a scale to measure cognitive distortions in bulimia. *Journal of Personality Assessment, 50,* 630–639.

Secord, P. F., & Jourard, S. M. (1953). The appraisal of body-cathexis: Body-cathexis and the self. *Journal of Consulting Psychology, 17,* 343–347.

Shontz, F. C. (1974). Body image and its disorders. *International Journal of Psychiatry in Medicine, 5,* 461–472.

Silberstein, L. R., Striegel-Moore, R. H., & Rodin, J. (1987). Feeling fat: A woman's shame.

In H. B. Lewis (Ed.), *The role of shame in symptom formation*. Hillsdale, NJ: Lawrence Erlbaum Associates.

Silberstein, L. R., Striegel-Moore, R. H., Timko, C., & Rodin, J. (1988). Behavioral and psychological implications of body dissatisfaction: Do men and women differ? *Sex Roles, 19,* 219–231.

Silverstein, B., Peterson, B., & Perdue, L. (1986). Some correlates of the thin standard of bodily attractiveness for women. *International Journal of Eating Disorders, 5,* 895–906.

Silverstein, B., Perdue, L., Peterson, B., & Kelly, E. (1986). The role of the mass media in promoting a thin standard of bodily attractiveness for women. *Sex Roles, 14,* 519–532.

Simmons, R. G., Blyth, D. A., & McKinney, K. L. (1983). The social and psychological effects of puberty on white females. In J. Brooks-Gunn & A. C. Petersen (Eds.) *Girls at puberty* (pp. 229–278). New York: Plenum Press.

Skrinar, G. S., Bullen, B. A., Cheek, J. M., McArthur, J. W., & Vaughan, L. K. (1986). Effects of endurance training on body-consciousness in women. *Perceptual and Motor Skills, 62,* 483–490.

Slade, P. D. (1977). Awareness of body dimensions during pregnancy: An analogue study. *Psychological Medicine, 7,* 245–252.

Slade, P. D. (1985). A review of body-image studies in anorexia nervosa and bulimia nervosa. *Journal of Psychiatric Research, 19,* 255–265.

Slade, P. D., Dewey, M. E., Newton, T., Brodie, D., & Kiemle, G. (in press). Development and preliminary validation of the Body Satisfaction Scale. *Psychology and Health.*

Slade, P. D., & Russell, G. F. M. (1973). Awareness of body dimensions in anorexia nervosa: Cross-sectional and longitudinal studies. *Psychological Medicine, 3,* 188–199.

Speaker, J. G., Schultz, C., Grinker, J. A., & Stern, J. S. (1983). Body size estimation and locus of control of obese adolescent boys undergoing weight reduction. *International Journal of Obesity, 7,* 73–83.

Stelnicki, G., & Thompson, J. K. (1989). Eating disorders in the elderly. *The Behavior Therapist, 12,* 7–9.

Strauss, J., & Ryan, R. M. (1988). Cognitive dysfunction in eating disorders. *International Journal of Eating Disorders, 7,* 19–28.

Striegel-Moore, R. H., McAvay, G., & Rodin, J. (1986). Psychological and behavioral correlates of feeling fat in women. *International Journal of Eating Disorders, 5,* 935–947.

Striegel-Moore, R. H., Silberstein, L. R., & Rodin, J. (1986). Toward an understanding of risk factors for bulimia. *American Psychologist, 41,* 246–263.

Strober, M. (1981). The relation of personality characteristics to body image disturbance in juvenile anorexia nervosa: A multivariate analysis. *Psychosomatic Medicine, 43,* 323–330.

Stunkard, A., & Burt, V. (1967). Obesity and the body image: II. Age of onset of disturbances in the body image. *American Journal of Psychiatry, 123,* 1443–1447.

Stunkard, A. J., Sorenson, T., & Schlusinger, F. (1983). Use of the Danish adoption register for the study of obesity and thinness. In S. S. Kety, L. P. Rowland, R. L. Sidman, & S. W. Matthysse (Eds.), *The genetics of neurological and psychological disorders* (pp. 115–120). New York: Raven Press.

Taylor, M. J., & Cooper, P. J. (1986). Body size overestimation and depressed mood. *British Journal of Clinical Psychology, 25,* 153–154.

Thompson, J. K. (1986, April). Larger than life. *Psychology Today, 24,* 38–44.

Thompson, J. K. (1987a). Body size distortion in anorexia nervosa: Reanalysis and reconceptualization. *International Journal of Eating Disorders, 6,* 379–384.

Thompson, J. K. (1987b). Behavioral and cognitive-behavioral treatment of anorexia nervosa and bulimia nervosa: Current status, circa 1986. *Behavior Modification, 11,* 395–397.

Thompson, J. K. (1988a). Similarities among bulimia nervosa patients categorized by current and historical weight. *International Journal of Eating Disorders, 7,* 185–190.

Thompson, J. K. (1988b). Clinical exchange: It's My Face. *Journal of Integrative and Eclectic Psychotherapy, 1,* 97–99.

Thompson, J. K. (1990). Body shape preferences: *Effects of instructional protocol and level of eating disturbance.* Unpublished manuscript.

Thompson, J. K. (in press). The make-up artist. In J. C. Norcross & N. Saltzman (Eds.), *Therapist wars: Contention and convergence in clinical cases.* New York: Jossey-Bass.

Thompson, J. K., Berland, N. W., Linton, P. H., & Weinsier, R. (1986). Assessment of body distortion via a self-adjusting light beam in seven eating disorder groups. *International Journal of Eating Disorders, 7,* 113–120.

Thompson, J. K., & Blanton, P. (1987). Diet, exercise, and energy conservation: A sympathetic arousal hypothesis of exercise dependence. *Medicine and Science in Sports and Exercise, 19,* 91–99.

Thompson, J. K., & Connelly, J. J. (1988). Experimenter gender and size estimation accuracy. *International Journal of Eating Disorders, 7,* 723–725.

Thompson, J. K., & Dolce, J. J. (1989). The discrepancy between emotional vs. rational estimates of body size, actual size, and ideal body ratings: Theoretical and clinical implications. *Journal of Clinical Psychology, 45,* 473–478.

Thompson, J. K., Dolce, J. J., Spana, R. E., & Register, A. (1987). Emotionally versus intellectually based estimates of body size. *International Journal of Eating Disorders, 6,* 507–514.

Thompson, J. K., Fabian, L. J., & Moulton, D. (1990). *A measure for the assessment of teasing history.* Unpublished manuscript.

Thompson, J. K., Penner, L. A., & Altabe, M. (1990). Procedures, problems, and progress in the assessment of body images. In T. F. Cash & T. Pruzinsky (Eds.), *Body images: Development, deviance, and change.* New York: Guilford.

Thompson, J. K., & Psaltis, K. (1988). Multiple aspects and correlates of body figure ratings: A replication and extension of Fallon and Rozin (1985). *International Journal of Eating Disorders, 7,* 813–818.

Thompson, J. K., & Spana, R. E. (1988). The adjustable light beam method for the assessment of size estimation accuracy: Description, psychometrics, and normative data. *International Journal of Eating Disorders, 7,* 521–526.

Thompson, J. K., & Spana, R. E. (1990). *Visuospatial ability and size estimation accuracy.* Unpublished manuscript.

Thompson, J. K., & Thompson, C. M. (1986). Body size distortion and self-esteem in asymptomatic, normal weight males and females. *International Journal of Eating Disorders, 5,* 1061–1068.

Thompson, J. K., & Williams, D. E. (1985). Behavior therapy in the 80's: Evolution, exploitation, and the existential issue. *The Behavior Therapist, 8,* 47–51.

Thompson, J. K., & Williams, D. E. (1987). An interpersonally-based cognitive-behavioral psychotherapy. In M. Hersen, R. M. Eisler, and P. M. Miller (Eds.), *Progress in behavior modification* (Vol. 21) (230–258). New York: Sage Publications, Inc.

Tobin-Richards, M., Boxer, A., & Petersen, A. C. (1983). Early adolescents' perceptions of their physical development. In J. Brooks-Gunn & A. C. Petersen (Eds.), *Girls at puberty* (pp. 127–154). New York: Plenum Press.

Touyz, S. W., & Beumont, P. J. V. (1987). Body image and its disturbance. In P. J. V. Beumont, G. D. Burrows, & R. C. Casper (Eds.), *Handbook of eating disorders* (pp. 171–187). New York: Elsevier Science Publishers.

Touyz, S. W., Beumont, P. J. V., & Collins, J. K. (1988). Does over- or underestimation of body shape influence response to treatment in patients with anorexia nervosa? *International Journal of Eating Disorders, 7,* 687–692.

Touyz, S. W., Beumont, P. J. V., Collins, J. K., & Cowie, I. (1985). Body shape perception in bulimia and anorexia nervosa. *International Journal of Eating Disorders, 4,* 261–265.

Touyz, S. W., Beumont, P. J. V., Collins, J. K., McCabe, M., & Jupp, J. (1984). Body shape perception and its disturbance in anorexia nervosa. *British Journal of Psychiatry, 144,* 167–171.

Traub, A. C., & Orbach, J. (1964). Psychophysical studies of body-image. 1. The adjusting body-distorting mirror. *Archives of General Psychiatry, 11,* 53–66.

Unger, R. K. (1985). Personal appearance and social control. In M. Safir, M. Mednick, I. Dafna, & J. Bernard (Eds.), *Women's worlds: From the new scholarship* (pp. 142–151). New York: Praeger.

Ward, T. E., McKeown, B. C., Mayhew, J. L., Jackson, A. W., & Piper, F. C. (1990). *The Body Cathexis Scale: Reliability and validity in an exercise setting.* Unpublished manuscript.

Wheeler, G. D., Conger, P., Wall, S. R., Belcastro, A. N., & Cumming, D. C. (1986). Are anorexic tendencies prevalent in the habitual runner? *British Journal of Sports Medicine, 20,* 77–81.

Whitaker, A., Davies, M., Shaffer, D., Johnson, J., Abrams, S., Walsh, B. T., & Kalikow, K. (1989). The struggle to be thin: A survey of anorexic and bulimic symptoms in a non-referred adolescent population. *Psychological Medicine, 19,* 143–163.

Williams, R. L., Schaefer, C. A., Shisslak, C. M., Gronwaldt, V. H., & Comerci, G. D. (1986). Eating attitudes and behaviors in adolescent women: Discrimination of normals, dieters, and suspected bulimics using the Eating Attitudes Test and Eating Disorder Inventory. *International Journal of Eating Disorders, 5,* 879–894.

Williamson, D. A., Davis, C. J., Bennett, S. M., Goreczny, A. J., & Gleaves, D. H. (in press). Development of a simple procedure for assessing body image disturbances. *Behavioral Assessment.*

Williamson, D. A., Davis, C. J., Goreczny, A. J., & Blouin, D. C. (1989). Body-image disturbances in bulimia nervosa: Influences of actual body size. *Journal of Abnormal Psychology, 98,* 97–99.

Willmuth, M. E., Leitenberg, H., Rosen, J. C., & Cado, S. (1988). A comparison of purging and nonpurging normal weight bulimics. *International Journal of Eating Disorders, 7,* 825–835.

Willmuth, M. E., Leitenberg, H., Rosen, J. C., Fondacaro, K. M., & Gross, J. (1985). Body size distortion in bulimia nervosa. *International Journal of Eating Disorders, 4,* 71–78.

Winstead, B. A., & Cash, T. F. (1984, March). *Reliability and validity of the Body Self-Relations Questionnaire: A new measure of body-image.* Paper presented at the Southeastern Psychological Association, New Orleans.

Wooley, S. C., & Kearney-Cooke, A. (1987). Intensive treatment of bulimia and body-image disturbance. In K. D. Brownell, & J. P. Foreyt (Eds.), *Handbook of eating disorders: Physiology, psychology, and treatment of obesity, anorexia, and bulimia.* New York: Basic Books.

Wooley, S. C., & Wooley, O. W. (1984, February). Feeling fat in a thin society. *Glamour,* 198–252.

Yates, A., Leehey, K., & Shisslak, C. M. (1983). Running—an analogue of anorexia? *The New England Journal of Medicine, 308,* 251–255.

Zellner, D. A., Harner, D. E., & Adler, R. L. (1989). Effects of eating abnormalities and gender on perceptions of desirable body shape. *Journal of Abnormal Psychology, 98,* 93–96.

Appendix A

Obligatory Exercise Questionnaire

Directions: Listed below are a series of statements about people's exercise habits. Please circle the number that reflects how often you could make the following statements:

1 – NEVER   2 – SOMETIMES   3 – USUALLY   4 – ALWAYS

1. I engage in physical exercise on a daily basis. 1 2 3 (4)

2. I engage in one or more of the following forms of exercise: walking, jogging/running, or weightlifting. 1 2 3 (4)

3. I exercise more than three days per week. 1 2 3 (4)

4. When I don't exercise I feel guilty. 1 2 3 (4)

5. I sometimes feel like I don't want to exercise, but I go ahead and push myself anyway. 1 (2) 3 4

6. My best friend likes to exercise. 1 (2) 3 4

7. When I miss an exercise session, I feel concerned about my body possibly getting out of shape. 1 2 (3) 4

8. If I have planned to exercise at a particular time and something unexpected comes up (like an old friend comes to visit or I have some work that needs

immediate attention) I will usually skip my exercise for that day.   1 (2) 3 4

9. If I miss a planned workout, I attempt to make up for it the next day.   1 2 3 (4)

10. I may miss a day of exercise for no good reason.   (1) 2 3 4

11. Sometimes I feel a need to exercise twice in one day, even though I may feel a little tired.   1 (2) 3 4

12. If I feel I have overeaten, I will try to make up for it by increasing the amount I exercise.   1 (2) 3 4

13. When I miss a scheduled exercise session I may feel tense, irritable, or depressed.   1 2 3 (4)

14. Sometimes I find that my mind wanders to thoughts about exercising.   1 (2) 3 4

15. I have had daydreams about exercising.   1 (2) 3 4

16. I keep a record of my exercise performance, such as how long I work out, how far or how fast I run.   (1) 2 3 4

17. I have experienced a feeling of euphoria or a "high" during or after an exercise session.   1 2 3 (4)

18. I frequently "push myself to the limits."   1 2 (3) 4

19. I have exercised even when advised against such activity (i.e. by a doctor, friend, etc.).   1 (2) 3 4

20. I will engage in other forms of exercise if I am unable to engage in my usual form of exercise.   1 2 (3) 4

Note: Information regarding scoring criteria, norms, and psychometric data for the Obligatory Exercise Scale, Teasing Assessment Scale (Appendix B), and Body Image Anxiety Scale (Appendix C) may be obtained by writing J. Kevin Thompson, Ph.D. at the address given below:

J. Kevin Thompson, Ph.D.
Department of Psychology
University of South Florida
Tampa, Florida 33620

Appendix B

Teasing Assessment Scale

Directions: Each question pertains to the time period when you were growing up. Please respond by circling the appropriate number for the following scale: 1 = Never; 5 = Frequently.

	Never			Frequently	
1. Were you ridiculed as a child about being overweight?	1	2	3	4	5
2. Did other kids ever make jokes about your hair?	1	2	3	4	5
3. Did people used to point you out of a crowd because of your weight?	1	2	3	4	5
4. Did other kids call you derogatory names that related to your size or weight?	1	2	3	4	5
5. When you were a child, did you feel that your peers were staring at you because you were overweight?	1	2	3	4	5
6. Did other kids tease you about wearing clothes that didn't match or were out of style?	1	2	3	4	5

	Never			Frequently	

7. When you were a child, did you ever feel like people were making fun of you because of your weight? 1 2 3 4 5

8. Did your family grin or smirk when you asked for additional helpings of food? 1 2 3 4 5

9. Did your mother ever tell you that you wouldn't be able to "catch a man" because of your weight? 1 2 3 4 5

10. Did your family make you feel uncomfortable because of physical changes during puberty? 1 2 3 4 5

11. Did your brother(s) or other male relatives call you names like "fatso" when they got angry at you? 1 2 3 4 5

12. When you were a child were you scoffed at for looking like a weakling? 1 2 3 4 5

13. Did your parents or teachers ever tell you that you would never be a success because of your weight? 1 2 3 4 5

14. When you were a child, were you laughed at for trying out for sports because you were heavy? 1 2 3 4 5

15. Did your father ever make jokes that referred to your weight? 1 2 3 4 5

16. Did you ever hear your classmates snicker when you walked into the classroom alone? 1 2 3 4 5

17. When you were growing up, did people say you dressed funny? 1 2 3 4 5

18. Were you the brunt of family jokes because of your weight? 1 2 3 4 5

	Never			Frequently	
19. Did you ever feel like people were pointing at you because of your size or weight?	1	2	3	4	5
20. Did people used to say you had funny teeth?	1	2	3	4	5
21. Did other kids ever laugh at you because of the frequency or amount that you ate?	1	2	3	4	5
22. Did kids call you funny looking?	1	2	3	4	5
23. When you were a child, did people used to make jokes about your being too big?	1	2	3	4	5

Appendix C

Body Image Anxiety Scale

(TRAIT)

The statements listed below are to be used to describe how anxious, tense, or nervous you feel <u>IN GENERAL</u> (that is, usually), about your body or specific parts of your body.

Please read each statement and choose the answer which best indicates the extent to which each statement holds true <u>IN GENERAL</u>. Remember, there are no right or wrong answers.

0	1	2	3	4
never	rarely	sometimes	often	almost always

<u>IN GENERAL</u> I feel <u>anxious</u>, <u>tense</u>, or <u>nervous</u> about:

1. The extent to which I look overweight	0	1	2	3	4
2. My thighs	0	1	2	3	4
3. My buttocks	0	1	2	3	4
4. My hips	0	1	2	3	4
5. My stomach (abdomen)	0	1	2	3	4
6. My legs	0	1	2	3	4
7. My waist	0	1	2	3	4

8. My muscle tone	0	1	2	(3)	4
9. My ears	0	1	(2)	3	4
10. My lips	0	1	(2)	3	4
11. My wrists	0	1	(2)	3	4
12. My hands	0	1	2	(3)	4
13. My forehead	0	1	(2)	3	4
14. My neck	0	1	(2)	3	4
15. My chin	0	1	(2)	3	4
16. My feet	0	1	2	(3)	4

(STATE)

The statements listed below are to be used to describe how anxious, tense, or nervous you feel about your body or specific parts of your body right now (while you imagine yourself in the situation I just described).

Please read each statement and choose the answer which best indicates the extent to which each statement holds true IF YOU WERE ACTUALLY IN THE SITUATION I DESCRIBED. Remember, there are no right or wrong answers.

0	1	2	3	4
not at all	slightly	moderately	very much so	exceptionally so

RIGHT NOW (IN THE SITUATION) I feel anxious, tense, or nervous about:

1. The extent to which I look overweight	0	1	2	3	(4)
2. My thighs	0	1	2	3	(4)

3. My buttocks	0	1	2	3	4
4. My hips	0	1	2	3	4
5. My stomach (abdomen)	0	1	2	3	4
6. My legs	0	1	2	3	4
7. My waist	0	1	2	3	4
8. My muscle tone	0	1	2	3	4
9. My ears	0	1	2	3	4
10. My lips	0	1	2	3	4
11. My wrists	0	1	2	3	4
12. My hands	0	1	2	3	4
13. My forehead	0	1	2	3	4
14. My neck	0	1	2	3	4
15. My chin	0	1	2	3	4
16. My feet	0	1	2	3	4

Instructions for High, Medium, and Low Conditions.

High—You are at the beach wearing a very revealing bathing suit—a two-piece suit. It is crowded and the beach is covered with people's towels and beach chairs. You are alone, taking a stroll by the edge of the water.

Medium—You have about a half-hour to kill between classes. It's Wednesday so on your way to class you take a stroll through the flea market.

Low—You are at home relaxing while watching your favorite TV show.

Appendix D

The Multidimensional Body-Self Relations Questionnaire

The following pages contain a series of statements about how people think, feel, or behave. You are asked to indicate the extent to which each statement pertains to you personally.

Your answers to the items in the questionnaire are anonymous, so please do not write your name on any of the materials. In order to complete the questionnaire, read each statement carefully and decide how much it pertains to you personally. Using a scale like the one below, indicate your answer on the computerized answer sheet by blackening the appropriate circle to the right of the number of the statement.

A	B	C	D	E
Definitely Disagree	Mostly Disagree	Neither Agree Nor Disagree	Mostly Agree	Definitely Agree

	A	B	C	D	E
EXAMPLE: I am usually in a good mood.	0	0	0	0	0

In the circle on the answer sheet, blacken an A if you definitely disagree with the statement; mark a B if you mostly disagree; mark a C if you neither agree nor disagree; mark a D if you mostly agree; or mark an E if you definitely agree with the statement.

There are no right or wrong answers. Just give the answer that is most accurate for you. Remember, your responses are anonymous, so please be <u>completely honest</u>. Please give an answer to all of the items. Check from time to time to make sure you are marking your answers on the correct item number on the answer sheet.

A	B	C	D	E
Definitely Disagree	Mostly Disagree	Neither Agree Nor Disagree	Mostly Agree	Definitely Agree

1. Before going out in public, I always notice how I look.

2. I am careful to buy clothes that will make me look my best.

3. I would pass most physical-fitness tests.

4. It is important that I have superior physical strength.

5. My body is sexually appealing.

6. I am not involved in a regular exercise program.

7. I am in control of my health.

8. I know a lot about things that affect my physical health.

9. I have deliberately developed a healthy lifestyle.

10. I constantly worry about being or becoming fat.

11. I like my looks just the way they are.

12. I check my appearance in a mirror whenever I can.

13. Before going out, I usually spend a lot of time getting ready.

14. My physical endurance is good.

15. Participating in sports is unimportant to me.

16. I do not actively do things to keep physically fit.

17. My health is a matter of unexpected ups and downs.

18. Good health is one of the most important things in my life.

19. I don't do anything that I know might threaten my health.

20. I am very conscious of even small changes in my weight.

21. Most people would consider me good-looking.

A	B	C	D	E
Definitely Disagree	Mostly Disagree	Neither Agree Nor Disagree	Mostly Agree	Definitely Agree

22. It is important that I always look good.

23. I use very few grooming products.

24. I easily learn physical skills.

25. Being physically fit is not a strong priority in my life.

26. I do things to increase my physical strength.

27. I am seldom physically ill.

28. I take my health for granted.

29. I often read books and magazines that pertain to health.

30. I like the way I look without my clothes.

31. I am self-conscious if my grooming isn't right.

32. I usually wear whatever is handy without caring how it looks.

33. I do poorly in physical sports or games.

34. I seldom think about my athletic skills.

35. I work to improve my physical stamina.

36. From day to day I never know how my body will feel.

37. If I am sick, I don't pay much attention to my symptoms.

38. I make no special effort to eat a balanced and nutritious diet.

39. I like the way my clothes fit me.

40. I don't care what people think about my appearance.

41. I take special care with my hair grooming.

42. I dislike my physique.

43. I don't care to improve my abilities in physical activities.

44. I try to be physically active.

45. I often feel vulnerable to sickness.

46. I pay close attention to my body for any signs of illness.

47. If I'm coming down with a cold or flu, I just ignore it and go on as usual.

A	B	C	D	E
Definitely Disagree	Mostly Disagree	Neither Agree Nor Disagree	Mostly Agree	Definitely Agree

48. I am physically unattractive.

49. I never think about my appearance.

50. I am always trying to improve my physical appearance.

51. I am very well coordinated.

52. I know a lot about physical fitness.

53. I play a sport regularly throughout the year.

54. I am a physically healthy person.

55. I am very aware of small changes in my physical health.

56. At the first sign of illness, I seek medical advice.

57. I am on a weight-loss diet.

For the remainder of the items use the response scale given with the item, and mark your answer on the computerized answer sheet as before:

58. I have tried to lose weight by fasting or going on crash diets.

A	B	C	D	E
Never	Rarely	Sometimes	Often	Very Often

59. I think I am:
   A. Very Underweight
   B. Somewhat Underweight
   C. Normal Weight
   D. Somewhat Overweight
   E. Very Overweight

60. From looking at me, most other people would think I am:
   A. Very Underweight
   B. Somewhat Underweight
   C. Normal Weight

A	B	C	D	E
Never	Rarely	Sometimes	Often	Very Often

D. Somewhat Overweight
E. Very Overweight

61–69. Indicate how satisfied you are with each of the following areas of your body.

A	B	C	D	E
Very Dissatisfied	Mostly Dissatisfied	Neither Satisfied Nor Dissatisfied	Mostly Satisfied	Very Satisfied

61. Face (facial features, complexion)

62. Hair (color, thickness, texture)

63. Lower torso (buttocks, hips, thighs, legs)

64. Mid torso (waist, stomach)

65. Upper torso (chest or breasts, shoulders, arms)

66. Muscle tone

67. Weight

68. Height

69. Overall appearance

Note: The *Multidimensional Body-Self Relations Questionnaire (MBSRQ)* has been developed through an extensive, iterative process of rational-empirical item selection and validation research, including factor-analytic research. Norms have been established based upon a stratified (sex-by-age distribution of the U.S. population) random sample from a survey of 30,000 respondents (Cash, Winstead, & Janda, 1986). The 69-item MBSRQ is now available as interactive computer software for testing, scoring, and normative profiling of individual clients and/or research subjects, including the creation of a raw data file (for statistical analysis) concurrent with data collection. Additional software is available to facilitate data entry, data file creation, and normative scoring of MBSRQs completed manually on answer sheets.

Scientists and practitioners interested in further information about the MBSRQ should contact Thomas F. Cash, Ph.D. at the address given below:

Thomas F. Cash, Ph.D.
Professor of Psychology
Old Dominion University
Norfolk, Virginia 23529-0267

Author Index

Subject Index

136

About the Author

J. Kevin Thompson is an associate professor of psychology in the Department of Psychology at the University of South Florida. He received his Ph.D. from the University of Georgia in 1982. He completed his internship at the University of Mississippi Medical Center and was a member of the Department of Psychiatry, University of Alabama in Birmingham and the Department of Psychology, Clemson University, prior to joining the University of South Florida in 1985.

His primary research and clinical interests are body image disturbance, eating disorders, psychotherapy integration, and psychotherapy assessment. Much of the material for this book stems from his own research and clinical work in the areas of body image and eating disorders. He has edited special issues of *Behavior Modification* and the *Journal of Cognitive Psychotherapy*. He has also served as an editorial reviewer for numerous journals and is on the editorial board of the *International Journal of Eating Disorders*. This is his first book.

Psychology Practitioner Guidebooks

Editors
Arnold P. Goldstein, Syracuse University
Leonard Krasner, Stanford University & SUNY at Stony Brook
Sol L. Garfield, Washington University in St. Louis

William L. Golden, E. Thomas Dowd & Fred Friedberg—
HYPNOTHERAPY: A Modern Approach

Patricia Lacks—BEHAVIORAL TREATMENT FOR PERSISTENT INSOMNIA

Arnold P. Goldstein & Harold Keller—AGGRESSIVE BEHAVIOR:
Assessment and Intervention

C. Eugene Walker, Barbara L. Bonner & Keith L. Kaufman—
THE PHYSICALLY AND SEXUALLY ABUSED CHILD: Evaluation and
Treatment

Robert E. Becker, Richard G. Heimberg & Alan S. Bellack—SOCIAL
SKILLS TRAINING TREATMENT FOR DEPRESSION

Richard F. Dangel & Richard A. Polster—TEACHING CHILD
MANAGEMENT SKILLS

Albert Ellis, John F. McInerney, Raymond DiGiuseppe & Raymond
Yeager—RATIONAL-EMOTIVE THERAPY WITH ALCOHOLICS AND
SUBSTANCE ABUSERS

Johnny L. Matson & Thomas H. Ollendick—ENHANCING CHILDREN'S
SOCIAL SKILLS: Assessment and Training

Edward B. Blanchard, John E. Martin & Patricia M. Dubbert—NON-DRUG
TREATMENTS FOR ESSENTIAL HYPERTENSION

Samuel M. Turner & Deborah C. Beidel—TREATING OBSESSIVE-
COMPULSIVE DISORDER

Alice W. Pope, Susan M. McHale & W. Edward Craighead—SELF-
ESTEEM ENHANCEMENT WITH CHILDREN AND ADOLESCENTS

Jean E. Rhodes & Leonard A. Jason—PREVENTING SUBSTANCE
ABUSE AMONG CHILDREN AND ADOLESCENTS

Gerald D. Oster, Janice E. Caro, Daniel R. Eagen & Margaret A. Lillo—
ASSESSING ADOLESCENTS

Robin C. Winkler, Dirck W. Brown, Margaret van Keppel & Amy
Blanchard—CLINICAL PRACTICE IN ADOPTION

Roger Poppen—BEHAVIORAL RELAXATION TRAINING AND
ASSESSMENT

Michael D. LeBow—ADULT OBESITY THERAPY

Robert Paul Liberman, William J. DeRisi & Kim T. Mueser—SOCIAL
SKILLS TRAINING FOR PSYCHIATRIC PATIENTS

Johnny L. Matson—TREATING DEPRESSION IN CHILDREN AND
ADOLESCENTS

Sol L. Garfield—THE PRACTICE OF BRIEF PSYCHOTHERAPY

Arnold P. Goldstein, Barry Glick, Mary Jane Irwin,
   Claudia Pask-McCartney & Ibrahim Rubama—REDUCING
DELINQUENCY: Intervention in the Community

Albert Ellis, Joyce L. Sichel, Raymond J. Yeager, Dominic J. DiMattia,
Raymond DiGiuseppe—RATIONAL-EMOTIVE COUPLES THERAPY

Clive R. Hollin—COGNITIVE-BEHAVIORAL INTERVENTIONS WITH
YOUNG OFFENDERS

Margaret P. Korb, Jeffrey Gorrell & Vernon Van De Riet—GESTALT
THERAPY: Practice and Theory, Second Edition

Donald A. Williamson—ASSESSMENT OF EATING DISORDERS:
Obesity, Anorexia, and Bulimia Nervosa

J. Kevin Thompson—BODY IMAGE DISTURBANCE:
Assessment and Treatment